21ST-$\mathscr{C}$ENTURY
CELLISTS

STRING LETTER PUBLISHING

THORN

Publisher: *David A. Lusterman*
Editor: *Stacey Lynn*
Associate Editor: *Jessamyn Reeves-Brown*
Contributing Editor: *Mary VanClay*
Assistant Editor: *Matthew Kramer*
Production Director: *Ellen Richman*
Designer: *Trpti Todd*
Marketing Manager: *Jen Fujimoto*
Production Assistant: *Christopher Maas*
Contributors: *Richard Dyer, Edith Eisler, John Lehmann-Haupt, Andrew Palmer, Timothy Pfaff, Barbara Sealock*

Cover photographs: *front cover by J. Henry Fair courtesy ICM Artists; back cover (right) by Waring Abbott courtesy Columbia Artists Management and (left) by Marco Borggreve courtesy Channel Classics*

Printed in the United States of America.
All rights reserved. Produced by String Letter Publishing, Inc.
PO Box 767, San Anselmo, California 94979
(415) 485-6946; www.stringletter.com

Library of Congress Cataloging-in-Publication Data
21ST-century cellists/ [Stacey Lynn, editor].
        p.cm. -- (Backstage books)
            ISBN 1-890490-39-3
                1. Violoncellists--Interviews. I. Title: Twenty-first century cellists.
            II. Lynn, Stacey. III. Series.

ML398 .A1172001
787.4'092'2--dc21
[B]   00-054773

String Letter Publishing

Contents

Introduction

Properly titled, this volume of interviews and profiles would appear as *21st-Century Cellists, Teachers, Artistic Directors, Composers, and Musical Mentors.* Two strong themes run through this series of conversations.

First, there are no unidimensional musicians; even the mythic virtuosos, such as Paganini, led a multiplicity of simultaneous creative lives. Casanova, the well-known Venetian violinist (and arguably the first freelancer), is another notable historic figure. In this volume, you will encounter such contemporary examples as Yo-Yo Ma, Kermit Moore, Carlos Prieto, and Ralph Kirshbaum. Their need for personal, artistic, and intellectual challenges seems inexhaustible and may in fact be the source of their incredible energy and drive. Some inexplicable exceptions notwithstanding, musicianship could well turn out to be the sine qua non of the polymath.

Second, no musician is an island; indeed, the most compelling feature of musical culture, especially to its initiates, is the intimacy among students and teachers, performers and mentors, the majesty of traditions literally embodied in the generations. Painters and sculptors are as likely to reject as embrace their antecedents, and baseball Hall of Famers routinely bemoan their successors' ignorance of traditions, no matter how illustrious their on-field feats. But if you want to witness the miracle of transubstantiation, look no further than the ways in which musical values, ideas, and techniques are passed from one soul to the next. Hearing cellists such as Pieter Wispelwey and David Finckel describe the influence and power of teachers, coaches, mentors, and musical examples is to enter a world in which the potential and the actual seem in perfect balance.

Of course, the real world in which these musicians live and work is far from the ideal. So you will also learn of the challenges faced by young cellists such as Bion Tsang and Hai-Ye Ni, struggling to establish themselves as professionals and soloists, or of those confronting Kenneth Slowik, whose mission is to re-create and enliven historical performance practice in our day.

In short, these conversations with some of the 21st century's notable cellists take you immediately backstage, where you will hear their voices, their words, and their thoughts, unfiltered, unmediated, straight from the heart.

David A. Lusterman, Publisher

Kenneth Slowik

"I HAVE A DREAM," KENNETH SLOWIK concluded the following interview in 1994. His dream then was to record Richard Strauss' epochal 1945 *Metamorphosen,* for 23 strings, with instruments strung entirely in gut—no matter whether that was the way the piece was originally played. However radical, even backward, Slowik's idea may have seemed at the time, it has since become a reality on a Deutsche Harmonia Mundi CD—one that has earned him near-unanimous critical acclaim. His daring on disc hasn't hindered his podium prospects either. Guest-conducting dates in Spain and the U.S. have steadily increased, and he now holds two regular posts: conductor of the Santa Fe Bach Festival and the Santa Fe Pro Musica Chamber Orchestra, a combined period- and modern-instrument ensemble. Finally, his career as both a soloist and a chamber musician has continued. The Smithson Quartet discussed in this article eventually evolved into the Axelrod Quartet, which includes Slowik, violinists Ian Swenson and Marilyn MacDonald, and violist Steven Dann.

BEATING TIME

Timothy Pfaff

Asked to name his personal favorite from among his many prize-winning recordings—one he feels shows his playing at its most representative—cellist Kenneth Slowik takes an uncharacteristically long pause before settling on his performance on bass viol (with gamba colleague Jaap ter Linden) of Marin Marais' "Tombeau de Mr. Melton."

"I keep coming back to it," he responds, without so much as a nod to the deep eloquence of his own playing on the track. "It's terrific music—and in fact may be the source of the famous opening chorus of Bach's *St. Matthew Passion*. We know that Bach copied some of the works of François Couperin, and Couperin and Marais shared the same engraver. In prefaces by both of them you find apologies to the reader, as each waited for the engravers to be done with the other's music. We don't know that Bach saw Marais' work, but it seems quite likely that he might have. Anyway, here's Bach's big E-minor, 12/8 chorus," he volunteers, breaking into a fearless vocalization of "Wir setzen uns." "And in this tombeau," he continues, "in 4/4 and G minor, we have this," and he energetically intones a convincingly similar tune.

He makes his point in discourse that is pure Slowik—engaged, informed, imaginative, and spontaneously musical. Nor is it an accident that he has fixed on a recording in which he is a collaborative performer. Although the 39-year-old musician is no stranger to the recital platform—and has played solo engagements with orchestras including the Cleveland Orchestra and the Baltimore and National Symphonies—he has consolidated a reputation as a consummate ensemble musician. The director of the Chamber Music Program of the Smithsonian Institution's Division of Musical History since 1984, Slowik is better known to the listening public as the cellist of two of the division's resident ensembles, the Smithson String Quartet and the Castle Trio. Along with colleague Anner Bylsma, he is also a cellist on the revelatory series of recordings that Sony Classical, on its Vivarte imprint, is issuing, featuring the exemplary Stradivaris of the Smithsonian Collection of Instruments (for which Slowik has curatorial responsibilities).

The opportunity to perform and record on some of the world's finest instruments is a privilege to which Slowik and his colleagues have responded with something approaching missionary zeal. Looking at the phenomenon another way, it is precisely the extent to which musicians use its instruments—a result in no small part of Slowik's distinctive curatorial style—that the Smithsonian's distinguished collection has fully realized its value. In a marked departure from the "through the glass darkly" style of instrument curatorship in many another institution, the Smithsonian literally broadcasts its holdings. "It's an optimal situation," Slowik points out, "that we can play our concerts in our wonderful, 200-seat Hall of Musical Instruments and, through radio broadcasts and recordings, reach audiences of hundreds of thousands. Through our extremely fortunate and good relationships with Deutsche Harmonia Mundi, Sony Classical, and Virgin Classics—as well as through our own Smithsonian Collection of Recordings—we have been able to fulfill that oft-quoted charge of the Smithsonian: 'Dedicated to the increase and diffusion of knowledge among men.'"

Slowik fondly recalls the day in 1980 that he introduced Bylsma to Washington, D.C.'s two Stradivari cellos ("strange that one city would have two of the surviving Strads that have not been cut down," he adds in a characteristic aside). "Before lunch he played the one at the Library of Congress, admitting that it was the first time he had played a Strad. I was shocked, until he explained that he had assiduously avoided it, afraid that the experience would make him dissatisfied with his own instruments—which are nothing to sneeze at: a Pressenda cello he uses for 19th- and 20th-century music and the Gofriller he uses for Baroque and Classical.

"When we got to the Smithsonian," Slowik continues, "the Hall of Musical Instruments was in use, so I took Anner and our 1701 Servais Strad into the adjacent Hall of Ceramics and Glass, where he played it. Some museum visitors gathered around to listen. After about 40 minutes, a guard came around to announce closing time. A woman who had been listening began asking Anner who he was—and what the beautiful instrument he was playing was—and, as he started answering her questions, tears spontaneously began running down his cheeks. He had been that moved by the experience. That is one of the great things about playing these instruments: we have them in our hands, and we know there is a direct link to the past. The feeling can be overwhelming."

In Slowik's case it was less than inevitable. Like many a conservatory student, he first set out to be an orchestra musician. As a student at the University of Chicago, he spent several years as cellist with Ralph Shapey's Contemporary Music Players, where playing a great deal of contemporary music—including Shapey's, after the composer lifted his own ban on the performance of his music—took him as far away from the world of "original instruments" as could be imagined: all the way to the world of the "prepared" cello, in fact. But his tale of playing a styrofoam-filled cello with an onboard speaker is a story for another day.

Chicago's vast popular-music culture afforded Slowik extensive experience as a session musician ("They brought in string players to 'sweeten' the sound," he recalls) and brought him in contact with musicians such as Sarah Vaughan, Frank Sinatra, and Tony Bennett. At the same time, but at the opposite pole of music making, he formed and led his own period-instrument ensemble, Fiori Musicali.

Although Slowik's interest in historical instruments was first piqued by harpsichords he built from kits (he remains an adept, natural performer at the keyboard to this day), the fascination quickly led to exploration of historical strings. Slowik now notes with a kind of wonder that he has not owned an instrument with metal strings since 1980. It is no accident that that was the watershed year a Fulbright Fellowship took him to Vienna, where he studied with Nikolaus Harnoncourt and performed with the Clemencic Consort.

Slowik's recollections of Harnoncourt focus on the famous cellist and conductor's "incredible charisma, which was sometimes so strong as to utterly overrule all kinds of musicological caution." In particular, Slowik cites an occasion on which he brought a Marais piece to one of Harnoncourt's master classes. Noting that Marais provided instructions on performing his music as detailed as any in the 18th century, Slowik reports that Harnoncourt responded to his master-class performance, which was along the lines Marais had specified, with "some very liberal suggestions. I found myself in that peculiar kind of out-of-body experience I had observed in so many of Harnoncourt's other students, finding myself similarly convinced by what he was saying. Only when the session was over did I come to grips with the fact that much of what he said contradicted the music. What I took away from Harnoncourt—whose work I still admire greatly—was less his particular point of view than the necessity for having a strong point of view on the music you perform."

At that time, the only two period-instrument recordings of Bach's solo cello suites were by Harnoncourt and August Wenzinger, another important influence on Slowik. When Anner Bylsma's famous Seon recording joined that company, Slowik recalls, "It set us all on our ears, so to speak. It was so fresh and free." His subsequent personal acquaintance with Bylsma led first to their collaboration as cellists on the award-winning Deutsche Harmonia Mundi recording of Boccherini's Op. 11 string quintets (performed on Stradivari instruments from the Smithsonian Collection), during which, Slowik says, "We hit it off. When I listen to that recording, I can tell immediately which one of us is playing, but another very good musician who was not at the sessions might not be able to tell."

Having concertized and recorded extensively with Bylsma since, in Europe as well as in America, Slowik himself now finds the distinction blurring. Sony Classical's recently released recording of Boccherini cellos sonatas with Bylsma also includes three Boccherini fugues for two equal cellos. "Even though it's only been a little more than a year since those sessions," Slowik comments, "when I hear it, sometimes even I don't know which of us is playing. It's been a very rich working relationship."

That could serve as a motto for Slowik's musical life as a whole. The Smithsonian chamber-music program Slowik oversees has recently reconfigured its resident ensembles into an entity known as the Smithsonian Chamber Music Society, which now showcases those ensembles in a freer mix of programs that also includes contributions from outside guests of the caliber of Bylsma, violinist Stanley Ritchie, and fortepianist Malcolm Bilson. (During the program's earlier days, many of today's front-ranking early-music specialists made their American debuts at the Smithsonian.)

Over recent years, however, Slowik and his parent institution have wisely concentrated their efforts on providing a solid foundation for the ensembles. The period of 11 years during which the Smithson String Quartet, for example, enjoyed stable personnel—Jaap Schröder and Marilyn McDonald, violins; Judson Griffin, viola; and Slowik—allowed the quartet to forge the kind of musical identity that has allowed for a smooth transition for its two new members, Jorie Garrigue and David Cerutti (replacing McDonald and Griffin). "Jaap and I have played nearly 50 of the 68 Haydn quartets together, as well as all the Mozarts and Beethovens and a number of Schuberts and Schumanns. So when we tackle a quartet we haven't done, there's a certain comfort. We've developed a unified approach. I want to stress how much I have enjoyed working with him and learned from him, but I also think that, as we work together longer and longer, the influence becomes mutual."

He finds the situation with the Castle Trio comparable, if yet more intense. "We are only three people, so it's even easier to work. When we get together, we simply let fly. We recently did Richard Strauss' wonderful early Piano Quartet, Op. 13, with violist Steven Dann, who has contributed to so much of the Smithsonian's ensemble work with Anner. But it was the first time Steven had worked with my trio colleagues, Marilyn McDonald and fortepianist Lambert Orkis. After one of the rehearsals, he told me how good it was that no one was afraid to say anything to another member of the trio. In reality, there's so little ego involved that we are free to say, 'That sounds like a pig,' or 'Can't you try thus and so?' Put more positively, we have developed our own vocabulary, so when one of us says, 'a spike there,' we all know what we mean. When three people put their minds together, a synergy develops, so there is something almost electric, to use a trite word. The sparks do fly from time to time."

The trio's method also involves a flexibility of musical approaches. Among its debut discs, on the Smithsonian's own label, was its 1988 traversal of Beethoven's Op. 70 trios. "At that time we consciously followed what Czerny had to say about Beethoven style in his famous argument with Anton Schindler," Slowik explains. "To boil the argument down, perhaps a little too much, Schindler was for all sorts of agogic freedoms, while Czerny kept saying '*Nicht schleppend*, don't drag, stay in tempo.' There's a lot to be said for the Czernian approach, and any number of critics noted that we hewed to it on that recording." The Castle Trio's complete Beethoven trio cycle for Virgin Classics, now nearly complete, affords the musicians a second opportunity to record Op. 70. "We'll do it differently now," Slowik promises. "We have added a liberal amount of time taking here and there—but the Czernian approach has provided us with a kind of backbone, not a rigidity but a certain kind of structural support.

"If I had to say what excited me most about having time to work a piece out, it's that when everyone understands the structure, or at least shares a view of the structure, then the piece begins to unfold for the listener in a way that might otherwise not have been as immediately apparent. It gives the piece conviction. Holding back a little at the introduction of the second theme in a sonata-form movement, for example, not only gives a nice ebb and flow to the piece, it also coolly brings out when the music is moving from one section to another. That's something we don't have so much of any more, particularly in recordings, which seem to have become more metronomic.

"The process of working all this out is what's so interesting, and what my colleagues would agree serves as a kind of life belt. When we go out on stage, no matter how we feel, individually or collectively—no matter whether the hall is reverberant or dry—what guides us is that extensive working-out period. I'm tempted to call it a luxury, but I think it's really a great necessity."

Ample preparation time, the kind of rehearsal period that allows "careful" preparation—so that the performance doesn't sound careful—is what excites Slowik about conducting, which occupies a steadily increasing amount of his musical life. To date, the best representation of his conducting on CD is my personal favorite among the various historically informed recordings of J.S. Bach's *St. John Passion*, a searching, thoroughly thought-out, stylistically impeccable, and deeply moving, interpretation. Its core musicians are Slowik's Smithsonian Chamber Players. Among its innovations is the deployment of a special 12-voice Smithsonian Chamber Chorus, each member of which sings not only the choruses and chorales but at least one of the name parts or solo arias as well. (Similarly, Slowik—playing both viola da gamba and cello—makes solo contributions to the arias.) One can practically hear the way thorough preparation time forged a unified vision out of the variety of individual musical contributions.

This April Slowik will lead—from one of the harpsichords in the continuo section—the Peabody Opera Studio's production of the final Monteverdi opera, *L'Incoronazione di Poppea*. "I like to have as much engagement from my colleagues as possible, and I've found that the best way to engender that is not by dictatorially slashing the air, beating time, but more by coaxing things out. The good thing about doing a project like this in a conservatory setting is not being hampered by mundane considerations—like having to pay people to participate—which means we can have unlimited rehearsals. That allows us to get closer to the piece than is often the case in modern concert reality. This may come from my chamber-music orientation, but I'm convinced that the more people understand what's going on, the more they sense what individual contributions they're making—and that's inevitably audible."

SELECTED RECORDINGS

(continued)

THE CELLO AND THE KING OF PRUSSIA. Works by Beethoven, Duport, Romberg, etc. With Stanley Hoogland, piano; Anner Bylsma, cello (Sony Classics 63360).

DOTZAUER: Pieces for Cello. With Anner Bylsma, Steven Doane, cellos (Sony Classical SK 64307).

DOTZAUER: Quintet for Strings. With Vera Beths, Jody Gatwood, violin; Lisa Rautenberg, viola; Anner Bylsma, cello (Sony Classical 64307).

MARAIS: Pièces à deux violes 1686 (Deutsche Harmonia Mundi 77146-2-RC).

MENDELSSOHN: Octet for Strings in E-Flat Major, Op. 20; Gade: Octet for Strings in F Major, Op. 17. With L'Archibudelli, Smithsonian Chamber Players (Sony Classics 48307).

continued...

The Peabody *Poppea*, an opera Slowik rightly deems "heavily reliant on text," will be sung in English, "for maximum immediacy." But more than language, Slowik's primary concern is, he says, "rhetoric—both the rhetoric of the music itself and the rhetoric of playing it accordingly. Imagine the most beautiful rhetorical statement, like a Shakespeare soliloquy, spoken poorly. What you get is only one shiver instead of ten. My interest is in making music a communicative medium and not just a pretty background—and that takes maximum communication among the musicians. It's when you get to know someone really well that you can really discourse."

WHAT HE PLAYS

In addition to the strings of the Smithsonian Collection of Instruments, which he curates, Kenneth Slowik performs on a number of instruments he owns. For music from about middle-period Beethoven on, he plays a cello by Carlo Antonio Testore, ca. 1750, with a modern neck but a slightly older-style bridge. For earlier music he plays a Paul François Grosset cello, made in Paris ca. 1748, which, Slowik says, "can accommodate things from a 415 setup to about 430 classical-pitch setup quite nicely." He also owns a Chapuis five-string violoncello piccolo, which he uses mostly for the Sixth Bach Suite but also for Bach cantatas. For much of the German repertoire he plays a Matthias Hümmel viola da gamba, made in Nürnberg in 1708. "Rather Stainer-esque in proportion," he says, "it's broad across the bottom and has original f-holes instead of c-holes." He also has a modern copy of a seven-string French viol by François Bodart. All of the above are strung with gut. The most recent addition to his cello family is "a beautiful 1696 Francesco Ruggeri instrument."

He owns an 18th-century bow ascribed to Edward Dodd of England, "a very beautifully made stick, rather overlong—an inch longer than a modern bow—with a nice swan's head on it. Although it's elegantly made, it draws a nice, full sound." He also has an anonymous bow, ca. 1730 or 1740, about an inch and a half shorter than a modern bow. Both, but particularly the shorter bow, have been successfully copied on several occasions. Since this article first appeared, Slowik has acquired additional bows by Bazin and Sartory. His ongoing work at the Smithsonian also gives him access to that institution's bow collection of cellist and gambist Janos Scholz, which he describes as "50 bows representing all periods of the bow's development, many of them in beautiful playing condition."

MOZART: Horn Quintet, K. 407; Flute Quartet, K. 285; Piano Quartets. With Lowell Greer, natural horn; Christopher Krueger, flute; J. Weaver, piano; Jaap Schröder, violin; J. Griffin, M. Graybeal, violas (Smithsonian Collection 5-ND 031).

THE NATURAL HORN. Haydn: Cassation for Four Horns and Strings in D Major; Divertimento for Two Horns and Strings in E-Flat Major; Concerto for Horn No. 1 in D Major; Divertimento for Horn, Violin, and Cello in E-Flat Major; Divertimento for Two Horns and Strings in D Major. With Ab Koster, natural horn; L'Archibudelli (Sony Classics 68253).

SCHUBERT: Quintet for Strings in C Major, Op. 163. With L'Archibudelli (Sony Classics 46669).

SPOHR: Double Quartet for Strings No. 1 in D Minor, Op. 65; Sextet for Strings in C Major, Op. 140; Quintet for Strings No. 2 in G Major, Op. 33, No. 2. With L'Archibudelli, Smithsonian Chamber Players (Sony Classics 53370).

Slowik's own flair for discourse that weds both musical and literary rhetoric reaches the public primarily by way of the program notes he supplies for almost every concert and recording in which he participates. Thoroughly informed musicologically—and in masterfully crafted prose—they are, like his music making, imaginative, involving, and unafraid of informed conjecture.

At a more expressly didactic level, Slowik channels his love of talking about music into teaching. A lecturer in performance practice at the University of Maryland since 1985, he also has served on the faculty of the prestigious Oberlin Baroque Performance Institute (BPI) since 1989. Having been associated with BPI in one way or another for 20 of its 23 years, he will become its director this summer. Characteristically, he relishes the opportunities of both "guiding the institute a little bit" and "preparing a few large pieces, some earlier 17th-century music."

Without forsaking his deep interest in early music, Slowik is emerging as one of the ranking generals in the performance-practice sally into the 19th century—until quite recently anathema to the early-music movement. He is involved in large-scale campaigns, Smithsonian projects such as the Beethoven piano-concerto project with his Castle Trio fortepiano colleague Orkis, as well as concert performances of all of Brahms' chamber music on period instruments prior to the composer's death centennial in 1997. And Slowik is also engaged, as both general and foot soldier, in a variety of fascinating border skirmishes. He and Bylsma are planning to record more 19th-century virtuoso cello music, for example. "There is just so much more 19th-century music that's available," Slowik proclaims, with faintly disguised avidity.

And then there's the 20th century. Last season the Castle Trio, no stranger to 19th-century music, took another step over the line by programming the Charles Ives Trio—"wonderfully funny," as Slowik recalls, "and also very moving. It was begun in 1904 and finished about 1911, so the piano we used was the Smithsonian's New York Steinway, an instrument [Ignacy] Paderewski played some 75 times. It worked very well. Some musicians were probably already using metal strings by that time, but we chose not to."

Slowik seems an exemplar of his generation—effectively, the third generation—of early-music specialists. Finely attuned to both the strengths and limitations of his historically inclined teachers and mentors, he seems less encumbered by the language that first defined but then ensnared his forebears—terms such as *authentic* and *original;* the word *movement* used to link what were really rival factions—and altogether more adept at speaking the polyglot mix that reflects the diverse national strata of historical music styles. Less obsessed with doing the "right" thing, and certainly not with being "righter-than-thou," Slowik enjoys the freedom to turn his own ever-deepening understanding of the musical past to the creation of a vital musical present.

"I have a dream," he confides, "and I only need to find out how to turn it into a reality. I want to perform and then record Richard Strauss' *Metamorphosen,* a 1945 work for 23 strings. Even though it may first have been performed with metal strings, I think it would sound terrific on gut. It's sort of a new twist on the old idea that if Bach had had a piano, he would have written music for it. But why not? We're not necessarily trying to claim that we're re-creating an original performing situation down to the last detail. We're trying to make this music speak to us."

Bion Tsang

2

SOLOIST AND CHAMBER MUSICIAN Bion Tsang began studying cello at age seven, and in his teens he became the youngest cellist to receive a Gregor Piatigorsky Memorial Prize, as well as being the youngest recipient of an Artists International Award. He has appeared with the New York Philharmonic, the Stuttgart Chamber Orchestra, the Moscow Philharmonic, and the Taiwan National Orchestra, among others. Building a career takes perseverance, as the following conversation, conducted in February 2000, reveals. Tsang works hard as a soloist, chamber musician, administrator, and teacher, and he manages to include his family in many of his activities. Having recently changed management, Tsang expects new engagements to keep him even busier in the coming seasons.

ENGAGING BION TSANG

Edith Eisler

I think it's in the nature of the music world that cellists are bound to have a very hard time building a solo career," says cellist Bion Tsang. He speaks from experience—he is one of those intrepid young performers who, through talent, brains, determination, and spunk, succeed in forging out a career virtually by their own efforts.

Encouraged by a close, supportive, music-loving family, Tsang studied with the best teachers and went to Harvard and Yale (where he met his future wife, fellow cellist Amy Levine, the daughter of bassist Julius and violist Caroline Levine). He was the youngest cellist to receive a Gregor Piatigorsky Memorial Prize, and he made his professional debut in two concerts with the New York Philharmonic under Zubin Mehta at age 11. In 1984, at age 17, he was chosen as a Presidential Scholar in the Arts by the National Foundation for the Advancement in the Arts, and he made his New York recital debut in the same year, as winner of the Artists International Award. He entered the Tchaikovsky Competition in Moscow twice, winning fifth prize in 1986 and a bronze medal in 1990; in 1992, he received an Avery Fisher Career Grant. Since then, he has appeared as soloist with orchestra, in recital, and in chamber music all over the world, and he has won a reputation as a champion of contemporary works, some of them written for him. He is also artistic director of the Laurel Festival of the Arts in Jim Thorpe, Pennsylvania.

I first heard him at a recital in Alice Tully Hall in 1992 and knew immediately that this was a player I wanted to hear again. His technique is brilliant but always at the service of the music, his tone is warm, beautiful, and variable, and his rhythm is flexible but controlled. His phrases have the natural flow of human speech, his melodies soar, and his response to the music is wonderfully spontaneous and expressive.

I spoke with him shortly after he had given the American premiere of George Enescu's Sinfonia Concertante, Op. 8, with the American Symphony Orchestra under Leon Botstein at Avery Fisher Hall. In the course of our conversation, I learned much about the trials, tribulations, and triumphs an aspiring young cellist encounters along the rocky road to a successful career.

Tell me something about your background and training.

Both of my parents are originally from China; they met in the States and I was born in Michigan. When I was six weeks old, my father got a job with IBM in Poughkeepsie, New York, and that's where I grew up. IBM, of course, stands for International Business Machines, but it used to be called "I've Been Moved," because they were always relocating their employees. My dad did get several such offers, but he refused them, because I entered the Juilliard Pre-College division in 1975, when I was eight; he wanted to make sure I could continue to go there.

I studied at Juilliard for nine years, first with Ardyth Alton, and then I also had the opportunity to study with Leonard Rose for about two years before he passed away. But I was a funny kid, and I wanted to stay with Alton as well. When I told Rose, he said, "That's fine," but he insisted that I also study with his assistant Channing Robbins. So I was taking lessons from all three of them at that point.

How did that work?

It worked very well for me, and they were all OK about it. I just took everything I could from each of them and incorporated it as well as possible. I don't remember getting any sort of conflicting information.

Did you study different pieces with each of them?

No, I wanted to see what they had to say about the same pieces. It was very interesting.

I'm sure it was. So you commuted from Poughkeepsie?

Yes, my father drove me [some 80 miles] every Saturday. I still have very vivid memories of driving in the snow, trying to get to Juilliard by 8:30 in the morning for the orchestra rehearsal. I'd sleep on the road, and my dad would sleep sitting in the car, waiting till parking became legal at 11 A.M.

What an accommodating father!

Yes, he certainly was. I had a very nice upbringing. My dad loved music; he always had it going in the house or was singing in the shower. I think he had wanted to be in the arts, but when his generation grew up in China, they pushed you into an area they thought would be good for you, and for him that was science. My mother wanted to be a journalist, but she gave that up to raise my brother and me.

Does your brother play as well?

He played piano and violin, but he was never serious. I think I might have discouraged him. I don't remember this, but my mother says that when I was very little, I would sit and listen to him practice and correct him. When I entered Juilliard, I progressed much more quickly than he did, so he decided to put his energies elsewhere.

Did you study before you went to Juilliard?

Just a year, in public school, where they started kids in third grade. My brother, who was older and to whom I was very close, already played the violin, so when it was my turn, I also wanted the violin, but the teacher said, "We need cellists in the orchestra; what about the cello?" I was undecided, but then his son, who was studying cello at Juilliard, gave a recital at our school, and I thought—yes, this is a good instrument. So in a way it was forced on me, but I accepted it and was very much encouraged.

With such good results that only four years later you played with the New York Philharmonic.

That's right. [*Laughs.*]

How did that come about?

Well, when [conductor Zubin] Mehta reinstituted the Young Performers' Competition that [Leonard] Bernstein had started, I auditioned for him and won that chance. I played the Boccherini Concerto—but only the first movement, because there were five of us, so each selection had to be short. But it was wonderful; Danny Kaye was host and I got to meet him. Later that year, Mehta invited me, along with two others, to play in another concert; I did the other two movements, so I got to perform the whole piece eventually!

The second concert was extra-special. It was 1980, the Year of the Child, and CBS did a huge production that was taped and televised worldwide—it was a big highlight of my life. I even got a concert out of it: a conductor from Reno saw the telecast and invited me to play.

How did you end up at Harvard?

After Juilliard, I really wanted to go to Yale, because my brother was there and both my parents had gone there, so I had a special feeling for it. But Aldo Parisot was teaching cello there, and I thought it would be awkward not to study with him, but I didn't want to leave Rose. So, following in the footsteps of Yo-Yo [Ma], I went to Harvard, where lessons are taken outside the university. As a music major, you study musicology and composition, but half your classes are in other fields, so I had a very broad liberal-arts education, which I very much appreciate.

Unfortunately, Rose passed away during my freshman year, but I continued to study with Channing Robbins and Ardyth Alton. At that point, I also began to study more with Luis Garcia-Renart, a Mexican cellist I had known for years, who lives in my hometown. He was a protégé of Casals and Rostropovich, two of my idols, and I'd often played for him. He sort of kept an eye on my career and eventually had perhaps the greatest influence on my playing.

You must have been in your first year at Harvard when you gave your New York debut recital.

Yes, just a week after Rose died, which was very sad. But I was lucky: this was when the *New York Times* still reviewed debuts at what was then called Carnegie Recital Hall, and I got a nice write-up, with a picture, too. The concert was a great success, my parents had managed to fill the hall, and the organizer was so impressed that he asked me back for another one. However, that one wasn't reviewed; I had to wait for my next *Times* review until the first time I played with the American Symphony and Leon Botstein, who always gets reviews because of his unusual programs.

After I graduated from Harvard, I spent a semester in London studying with William

Pleeth, and then I went to Yale for graduate school and studied with Parisot, but I made a point of taking some classes outside the music school.

And at Yale you met Amy.

Actually, I'd met her the summer before at Marlboro, and found out she was already at Yale. I looked her up, and then we happened to be stand partners in the first orchestra concert, and the rest, as they say, is history. We've been married for five years.

You must also still have been at Harvard when you first went to the Tchaikovsky Competition in Moscow.

Yes, in 1986; in 1990, I was at Yale. The first time I came out with the fifth prize, the second time with the third prize, the bronze. So I did better, and at the awards ceremony on stage, the head of the jury pulled me close to him and whispered in my ear, "Five, three, one"— implying that if I came back another time, I'd get the gold. But I felt twice was enough, and part of the reason was that, in 1990, I started to see that times were changing. In 1986, everything was extremely

well organized; the government was running the competition and had hired all the best orchestras and musicians. We played with the Moscow Philharmonic under Valery Gergiev, who was wonderful. In 1990, the competition was no longer sponsored by the government but by Pioneer Corporation, the electronics company; they wanted it run *their* way, and the old organization wanted it run their way, so there was a lot of chaos. Also, there was much less money; we had the Omsk Philharmonic, which was not very good, and neither was the conductor. It was quite a different experience, and I had a feeling it might be even worse in 1994.

What are the requirements for cellists?

The two pieces by Tchaikovsky, of course. The Pezzo Capriccioso is part of the first round, and the Rococo Variations part of the third round, with orchestra. In the second round, there is no Tchaikovsky, but they make sure you play at least one Russian piece. The first and second rounds are almost complete recital programs, and—unlike at many other competitions—they can't stop you. The third round is two concertos. It's a lot of music. In 1986, we had to learn a concerto by [Russian composer Tikhon] Khrennikov—but not on the spot, like at the Queen Elisabeth Competition. We got the music perhaps a month in advance. It only came with a piano reduction, no score, and everything was handwritten and very hard to decipher. I thought it was like that for all the contestants. But of course the Iron Curtain was still up, and when I arrived for the final round, I saw that the Russians had the score! In fact, I saw one of the Russian contestants being coached from the score by his teacher, who was a member of the jury, no less.

Was the concerto any good?

It was . . . OK. It was actually rather derivative.

Did you get anything out of winning these prizes?

Well, it's hard to say. I know that many Tchaikovsky laureates play a lot in Europe, and perhaps it was my fault that I didn't get a European manager immediately after the competition. I think that for a cellist, winning a prize is not as significant as for a pianist or a violinist. There are fewer cello competitions, to begin with. And a lot more attention is paid to the pianists and violinists; that was quite obvious at the Tchaikovsky. PBS came to do a documentary in 1986 and another television crew came in 1990; both went only to the violin and piano competitions and never showed up for the cellists.

But I have no doubt that winning those prizes in Moscow helped my career, just by getting my name out. To people who haven't heard you or worked with you, a bronze medal proves that your playing and your experience are on a certain level, and that's important for a freelance chamber musician. Besides, winning that prize probably helped me get the Avery Fisher Grant two years later.

Was that the only competition you ever entered?

Well, ever since I was a kid, that was the one I'd set my sights on; I always regarded it as the Olympics of music. When the Iron Curtain was up, there was an incredible mystique about the idea of a Westerner going behind it and, against all odds, coming back with a prize. Both times I was in Moscow, there were a lot of contestants—perhaps 80 or 90 cellists and as many as 130 pianists, and the level of playing was extremely high.

From what I've heard, most people try their wings, and steel their nerves, at some lesser contests before attempting the Tchaikovsky. You took on the musical Olympics right off, and won prizes, too! That's a remarkable achievement and must have required great courage. So what did you do after you left Yale?

I moved to New York, got engaged to Amy, and started on my professional career. In fact, my last two years at Yale were a sort of transition period between studying and performing; while I was doing the residency for my doctorate, I was also playing concerts. Before I graduated, and just after I got the Avery Fisher Grant, I signed on with one of the biggest concert agencies in the country. I'd rather not name it, because those people never really did anything for me. And it was ironic, because a contract with this management was another thing I'd wanted since I was a kid. So I was very excited when I got it, but I was naive, I didn't know the business, and I just got lost in the shuffle. They have so many big-name artists who demand their attention that they can't devote time to building careers.

Then why do they sign someone who's just starting out?

One reason that was suggested to me is that if my career would somehow all of a sudden take off, they'd be there to take the percentage—well, they say to push it, but really just to take the percentage.

So how did you get engagements?

Most of them I got for myself. For example, I'd play a concert in Taiwan with the guest conductor of the orchestra there, and then she'd invite me to her orchestra in America. So one thing would lead to another.

Did the management take a percentage even on the engagements you got on your own?

Sure, except that I made an agreement with them to make sure they wouldn't get anything on the chamber-music concerts. That was a good thing, because a large portion of my earnings has always come from those; I couldn't make a living without them.

But that's not why you do them, is it?

[*Laughs.*] No, of course not. Playing chamber music is a great joy to me, and luckily I'm at the point where I can pick and choose my concerts according to the repertoire and the other players. There's nothing like the miracle of different minds coming together to form one interpretation, one performance. I try to approach playing a concerto and interacting with the orchestra in the same way, except that you also have to project as a soloist a hundred percent of the time.

Tell me more about your chamber-music playing.

The bulk of it goes on during summer festivals, starting in May with my own festival. We do it so early in the summer because I can always be sure I'm available, and because there's no air-conditioning in the hall. We used to have it in June, but one year there was a huge heat wave and all of our instruments opened up. I've been involved with the festival for eight years, four of them as artistic director. It's a two-week affair, but for me it's obviously much longer, because I have to run the whole thing and do quite a bit of administrative work. But one of the joys of being in charge is that I get to invite the players.

Are they the same every year?

WHAT HE PLAYS

"For a good many years," says Bion Tsang, "I borrowed two different instruments, a 1705 Giovanni Grancino, and a Carlo Giuseppe Testore from 1700. When I entered college, my father bought me a cello made by Giovanni Bianchi in Florence in 1746, and though it doesn't project quite as well, it's nice to use something that feels as comfortable as an old shoe. I don't really have any good bows; I play on a Tubbs that actually belongs to Amy. It came with her cello, but then she found a very nice Sartory that she likes better, so I was given the Tubbs. In fact, Amy's cello sounds so great and powerful that I've sometimes wondered whether I should use it for important concerts, but I seem to have become more sensitive to change as I've grown older, and I can't adapt as quickly and easily as I used to. This is something [manager] Robert Levin is trying to work on—finding a sponsor to get me another instrument."

His strings are a Jargar forte A and medium D, and a Spirocore G and C, which are tungsten wound on steel. Tsang has interesting things to say about the importance of an instrument's setup. "The top of my cello is very soft," he said, "and the instrument almost got ruined by being set up too tightly. Then I found a man in Boston who loosened it and returned it to its natural state by putting in as short a soundpost as possible. Everything he does is based on balance. The strings are set up so the bridge and tailpiece are exactly centered, and the string length is exactly the same on the A and C strings. I remember the first time he set up my cello, before he even touched the bridge or the soundpost, he pulled the tailgut over a little bit and it made an enormous difference. It's amazing how much better these tiny little tweaks can make the instrument sound."

Some are; it depends on their schedules. Amy, of course, and one of my best friends who is in the San Francisco Symphony; I make a point of bringing him out every summer.

In June, I go to Alabama for a statewide festival. It's the same group every year with an occasional guest—Amy's come down for that one, for example.

It's in air-conditioned halls, I hope?

Oh, yes! But we do one outdoor pops concert, and that's an interesting experience. Your fingerboard becomes so slippery that it really teaches you control, so this is a good opportunity to try out some difficult repertoire: whatever you can play there, you can play anywhere. And besides, there are always bugs flying into your face.

From there, I go to the Seattle Chamber Music Festival, and then to Colorado for the Bravo! Vail Valley Festival. After that, I'm in Boston for my only regular teaching stint, at a three-week summer camp run by the Foundation for Chinese Performing Arts at the Walnut Hill School in Natick, Massachusetts. From there, I travel to play in other places, like Bargemusic in New York, Chestnut Hill in Connecticut, and Bridgehampton on Long Island. And that just about takes care of the summer.

Do you ever get a vacation?

I treat the whole thing as a working vacation, especially if Amy can be with me for part of it.

Do you play any chamber music the rest of the year?

Oh, sure. I'm often invited to join the Boston Chamber Music Society on its regular series and on tour, and I'm going to play with the New Jersey Chamber Music Society at the new Performing Arts Center in a huge cello concert titled Cellomania; Amy will be part of that. This year, my festival will be invited to appear at the Bethlehem Chamber Music Society, and I hope that will become a regular occurrence—so my summer festival will go on tour in the winter.

Do you play in Europe at all?

Well, recently I've been in Paris a few times at the invitation of a friend who lives there, the violinist Sasha [Alexandre] Brussilovsky. We met at a concert in California and since then I've asked him to my festival and he's asked me to his, Musicimes, in France. I also played on the

Normandy Coast in a Russian festival, where I premiered a work by Yuri Galperin, a very interesting composer.

Better than Khrennikov?

[*Laughs.*] Oh, yes! And next season I'm making my debut in Germany, then the following year I'm playing with the German Philharmonia of Westphalia. That was another of those chain reactions: its conductor came as guest to the Delaware Symphony when I was soloist and invited me. I've also made two recordings for a Paris-based label called Suoni e Colori: the Kodály Cello Solo Sonata and the Violin and Cello Duo with Brussilovsky, and the Piano Quartets of Strauss and [Joaquín] Turina, with Brussilovsky, Gennadi Freiden on viola, and Pascal Godart on piano.

I don't know the Turina—what's it like?

I love it; it's very passionate Spanish Gypsy music, really beautiful.

You seem to make a specialty of exploring out-of-the-way repertoire, like the Enescu Sinfonia Concertante I heard.

That's a good piece. It was one of several premieres I'm doing this season. In Boston, I'm pairing two in one concert: a concerto written for me by Noam Elkies, and the [Erich Wolfgang] Korngold Concerto, which was originally music for the film *Deception*.

Really! The script for that was written by my uncle, Joseph Than.

You're kidding! The music is very good; apparently people raved about it, so Korngold expanded it into a 13-minute piece. It's too bad he didn't go on to write a full-length concerto—it would have made a fine first movement—but it works very well on its own.

And Noam Elkies is an incredible man. He is probably one of today's foremost mathematicians and a real genius: graduated high school at 16, college at 18, got his doctorate at 20, wrote a doctoral dissertation that disproved maxims held for 200 years, and became the youngest tenured professor at Harvard. At the same time, he played the piano and still does; I played chamber music with him at Juilliard Pre-College, and he's apparently been composing since he was a child. I really admire his work and like what he writes: it's very classical in the sense that it has structure and motivic development, unlike a lot of music you hear today that seems just to paint scenes and string them together. In the last two years, I've done three of his pieces. This one is clearly influenced by Shostakovich, but he's like a chameleon and can write in any style, yet with a voice of his own.

Did you get all these engagements by yourself, too?

No, for the last couple of years I've had a new management, Performing Arts Consultants. Ironically, I met its president, Robert Levin, through my old management, and it's worked out really well. Robert is using this period to rebuild my career, which he feels was damaged by my name not having been out there for so many years. If you win a major prize and then are not heard of for a long time, people begin to think there's something wrong with you. So he's working on reintroducing me to a lot of orchestras and presenters and on getting me auditions with major conductors, where I've had a short but good track record: I played for Rostropovich, who hired me to play with the National Symphony, and for Zubin Mehta, under whom I appeared with the Chicago Civic Orchestra—though of course I had played for him much earlier, too. Robert also got me the engagement with the Delaware Symphony and the Enescu with Botstein. He's doing what the other management never did: getting me concerts in places where I've never been before, not just re-engagements.

Tsang plays with the New York Philharmonic, conducted by Zubin Mehta.

So things are moving! I'm looking forward to another busy summer and to more adventures next season.

Pieter Wispelwey

3

PIETER WISPELWEY GREW UP IN A MUSICAL household; his father was a violinist, and listening to string-quartet rehearsals was a regular part of the young cellist's boyhood. In 1985 he won first in the Elisabeth Everts Prize for the most promising musician in the Netherlands, and in 1992 he became the first cellist to receive the prestigious Netherlands Music Prize. A year after this 1996 interview, Wispelwey won the Belgian Press Prize for Musician of the Year, and his international career as a soloist is flourishing. The Bach Suites for Unaccompanied Cello have been integral to his repertoire—he began studying them at age ten, just as the early-music movement was taking off in Europe—and he has recorded the complete suites twice. However, his musical tastes are eclectic and he has performed and recorded pieces from Vivaldi to Schubert to Elliott Carter.

THE NEXT DUTCH MASTER

Richard Dyer

Boston is a cellists' town. Piatigorsky pupil Laurence Lesser is president of the New England Conservatory; Colin Carr teaches there, and Andrés Díaz is a few blocks away at Boston University. Yo-Yo Ma's home, and the staging area for his international career, is just across the river in Cambridge.

Several important cellists have stepped onto the world stage since Ma, but a charismatic young Dutchman named Pieter Wispelwey is the only one, so far, to have won a substantial following here in Boston, which is quite an achievement, considering that this town belongs to Yo-Yo Ma—and considering that Wispelwey has not yet appeared either with the Boston Symphony Orchestra or under the auspices of the prestigious Bank of Boston Celebrity Series.

This is how it happened. In the 1990–1991 season, having heard that Boston was a charming city, Wispelwey simply decided to present himself in three recitals in Jordan Hall. For a debut, all six Bach Suites for Solo Cello. Later he came back to play the Brahms sonatas on one program and all the Beethoven sonatas on the other—performances he decided to go through with even though his regular pianist, Paul Komen, had to return to the Netherlands because of a family emergency. Boston's leading collaborative pianist, Judith Gordon, deputized for the Brahms; Wispelwey contacted Lois Shapiro for the Beethoven at the suggestion of a mutual friend.

Those first concerts drew small but enthusiastic audiences—although not as small as the audience at Wispelwey's New York debut, the night before his first Boston appearance. "I played the Bach Suites in a Buddhist museum on a very steamy, hot day," he recalls. "There were 12 people there, including me and my manager! The audience was in one room and I was in the next, with a little fan."

With each appearance, Wispelwey's audience grew and favorable reviews accumulated. Now 33, Wispelwey has become a familiar and popular figure on the New England scene; he has played at Harvard, Wellesley, the Longy School of Music, and under the auspices of the Boston Early Music Festival. He also appears regularly with the New Hampshire Symphony and has become an annual visitor to Monadnock Music, a summer music festival that migrates among the small towns of southern New Hampshire. His many CDs have become local best-sellers. If Wispelwey can secure this degree of success in New England, the rest of America will surely follow. In fact, something like this pattern seems to have marked Wispelwey's conquest of the places that have become his other centers of activity; it is a career marked by considerable independence of mind.

The reasons for Wispelwey's popularity are clear. As critic Richard Buell, my colleague at the *Boston Globe,* wrote, "There is no more accomplished, imaginative, or exciting cellist before the public than Pieter Wispelwey, who knows old instruments and new, old music and new, and simply doesn't sound like anyone else." What has struck me about Wispelwey's performances, live and on record, is how detailed and personal they are. The most strikingly individual aspect of his playing is his approach to vibrato, which for him is not a uniform and automatic expressive device. Instead he uses many speeds and spreads of oscillation to impart a unique "speaking" quality to the singing quality that is the most prized characteristic of his instrument. In Wispelwey's hands, the cello no longer plays songs without words; he is a profoundly communicative musician.

On stage, Wispelwey is an intense, romantically handsome, yet utterly businesslike figure—paradoxical qualities that carry over from his offstage personality, which is quiet, serious, quirky, charming, and very intense indeed.

His first instrument, he will tell you, was the piano, which he began studying at four; he says he wasn't big enough to take up the cello until he was eight. His piano teacher, Dicky Boeke, became his first cello teacher, and Wispelwey kept up with the piano through his teenage years. His musical training was thorough, because he thought his goal was to become not an instrumentalist but a composer. "I wrote a lot of stormy music in C minor," Wispelwey says with a grin, "but it was only a hobby, something I was doing for myself. I soon gave it up."

Virtually from the beginning of his studies, Wispelwey was interested in the widest range of musical expression—in Baroque and Renaissance music, in Bruckner and Wagner, and above all in the central tradition of German *Lieder*—Schubert, Schumann, Brahms, Strauss, and Wolf. As a teenager, Wispelwey heard the German baritone Dietrich Fischer-Dieskau sing five recital programs, including Schubert's "Winterreise." "It is impossible to describe the power of how he sang in concert—it was so rich, controlled, expressive, elevated, and immediate."

Wispelwey was also interested from the start in working with other musicians of independent habits of mind. It was this that attracted him to Lois Shapiro, who has become his most frequent collaborator in his American concerts. "Her way of thinking, of rehearsing, of making music is for me so much more inspiring than to work with some cello god like Janos Starker. I am not interested in dogma or rigid opinion. Lois is always challenging, asking questions, utterly critical of herself, and of me, and I enjoy that very much. It is out of the question to be

on the defensive when the issue is to find a way to make a phrase convincing."

Wispelwey became interested in historical performance practice at a very early age. "This was part of my education, growing up in Amsterdam. Dicky Boeke's oldest son is a recorder player and gambist who was a student of Frans Brueggen's, and toured the States and Australia with Brueggen's ensemble Sour Cream. This was part of the world I was in. I heard [singer] Alfred Deller doing concerts in Amsterdam."

The great figure in historical cello studies, of course, is another Dutchman, Anner Bylsma. Hearing Bylsma for the first time changed Wispelwey's life. "I heard him play the Bach Suites in a church in the middle of Amsterdam when I was still a child—it must have been in 1976. I couldn't sleep for a week. I still carry around with me the sound of his piccolo cello. To see that solitary person creating this world, speaking this language, unfolding this mystery—it was all so meaningful."

A few years later, in 1981, Wispelwey began a close musical association with Bylsma, which lasted for four crucial years; but like many other master-disciple relationships, this one ended badly. "I never played Bach for him," Wispelwey emphasizes. "I was afraid of copying his playing." Wispelwey won't go into the problems with Bylsma in detail, but he indicates that the reasons for the "violent" breach were both personal and musical, and he closes the subject by saying, "I haven't seen him for eight years, and I have not felt the desire to."

After leaving Bylsma's circle in 1985, Wispelwey fulfilled a long-standing wish when he came to America to study with Paul Katz of the Cleveland Quartet at the Eastman School of Music. A scholarship from the Rotary Foundation made it possible. "It was important for me to come abroad," Wispelwey says. "In Amsterdam, we were completely isolated in Bylsma's world. Now I was living in an American downtown, participating in the life of a great university, and I had a real social life. I could also

SELECTED RECORDINGS

BACH: Six Suites for Cello Solo (CCS 1090 and CCS 12298).

BEETHOVEN: Complete Sonatas for Pianoforte and Cello (CCS 3592).

BEETHOVEN: Variations for Violoncello and Pianoforte. With Lois Shapiro, piano (CCS 6494).

BRAHMS: Sonata in E Minor; Sonata in F Major. With Paul Komen, piano (CCS 5493).

CELLO. Music by Elgar, Lutoslawski (CCS 12998).

DVORAK: Cello Concerto in B Minor; Rondo in G Minor. (CCS 8695).

HAYDN: Cello Concertos in C Major, D Major (CCS 7395).

continued...

practice without distraction for eight hours a day—there's not even a zoo in Rochester. I thought I was in paradise!"

Another important influence on Wispelwey's development was Colin Carr, who from his own teenage years regularly performed in Holland. "Colin represented something utterly different from what I was used to, a convincing musical alternative to Bylsma's world. Colin had a completely different attitude toward personal musical expression; he comes out of the world of English playing represented by William Pleeth, and it is a far more emotional kind of playing than what Bylsma represents. I also learned all about Boston from Colin; it

WHAT HE PLAYS

Pieter Wispelwey's instrument for his early-music performances and recordings is a Barak Norman cello, built in London in 1710. "I use it for everything up to the Brahms Sonatas," he says. "I first saw it standing in a corner at a dealer's, and I asked if I could use it for a concert, and after I did, I knew I had to buy it. When I first tried the cello, I heard a sound I had never heard before—it comes from the low tension on the strings. It is particularly wonderful in early-Romantic music—like an opera singer. It's a very light instrument; it doesn't weigh anything, and the upper blade is dangerously thin, although there is an extra curl in the neck that is very nice. There are some strange things about it—some restorations inside, perhaps. The body of the instrument is very broad, a very dark, dark brown, and threatening—it makes me think of a bear." He adds that Yo-Yo Ma has borrowed the cello for some of his own Haydn Concerto performances in Amsterdam.

The piccolo cello Wispelwey uses in the Sixth Bach Suite is a 7/8-size cello from 1770 "by that famous builder Anonyme," Wispelwey says, adding, "He was a great painter also!" He explains, "This is not a five-string cello, but I am thinking about changing it for that by making the fingerboard broader. It is such a delightful instrument."

Wispelwey's modern cello is a French instrument built in 1870, "also by Anonyme." He admits, however, that he is on the lookout for another instrument—and for sponsors to help him pay for it. He speaks with special fondness of a Grancino owned by a member of the Orpheus Quartet, which seemed to me ideal in size, atmosphere, and audience for what I wanted to do."

Meanwhile the proprietors of a young Dutch record company called Channel Classics approached Wispelwey and invited him to record anything he wanted to. At 26, he started off with the Bach Solo Suites. "I didn't think it was such a big deal. It's only two hours of music, after all—little pieces. The music is so pure, what Bach did—it is not tormented; it is almost naive, in a beatific kind of way. I'm very happy I started off with Bach, and now I hope to record the Suites all over again. I learned a lot from the experience of recording them."

he heard when he joined the quartet for a performance of the Schubert Quintet. "That Grancino was the best cello I ever heard." In some of his New Hampshire concerts, Wispelwey has played a new cello, a copy of a Gofriller, by the Boston craftsman Michele Ashley. "That is an exquisite instrument, very fresh."

Wispelwey's interest in historical performance practice led him to prefer playing the modern cello with gut strings until the late 1980s. He has changed his mind and no longer insists on this, for two reasons. First, certain major contemporary works that Wispelwey loves, by Shostakovich and Dutilleux, were written for steel strings, and they are scarcely practicable on gut. Also, Wispelwey says, "I don't love perfectionism for its own sake. I got very tired of taking risks, of going out of tune, of making funny noises."

Wispelwey prefers French bows. "For years I used a Satory, but now I use a Bazin, which has more resonance. I use a Dodd bow for Haydn and for the Beethoven Sonatas. It's a very funny bow, long and extremely heavy, but you don't feel that when you're playing. It has a very peculiar kind of elegance."

Wispelwey says he has never played a "tremendous" instrument that could fulfill his every fantasy. He has his eye on a Guarneri cello and is trying to arrange sponsorships to buy it. "I need a new inspiration, a partner, but always it is the alchemist's struggle, the effort to make gold out of wood!"

Asked to expand on this point, Wispelwey says, "For me, recording was an enormous step toward achieving greater control. Listening to recordings of yourself is the most immediate way you have of improving your playing, because you hear everything. You are taught as a musician to listen to yourself while you're playing, but the discrepancy between what you hear when you're playing and what you hear on a recording is horrifying. I am certain that is why the technique of instrumental playing has improved such a lot. When you listen to early concert performances by Mstislav Rostropovich, his playing is not nearly as flawless as it later became. That must have come from his recording experience."

Since Wispelwey's debut recording, he has made a substantial start on setting down the complete mainstream cello repertory for Channel. He has recorded the Beethoven and Brahms sonatas with Komen, the Beethoven Variations with Shapiro, the Vivaldi sonatas and Haydn concertos with the original-instrument group Florilegium. For another label, Globe, he began a survey of the major 20th-century classics, two CDs including solo sonatas by Britten, Kodály, Escher, and Crumb. Now Channel has taken over that dimension of his recording activity, too; Wispelwey's most recent release is of solo works by Ligeti (Sonata), Hindemith (Sonata), Roger Sessions (*Six Pieces*), Peter Sculthorpe (Requiem), and Chiel Meijering (*La Belle Dame Sans Merci*). Last winter Wispelwey recorded the Dvořák Concerto live with the Netherlands Philharmonic; he hopes it will be released this spring.

"I am also very interested in all the music that is not yet written," Wispelwey adds confidently. "Young composers are now coming to me, so I first challenge them to write some gestures for me—30-second phrases, rhythms, pieces, then maybe some études or caprices. It is important to add to the everyday repertoire. Chiel Meijering did write a concerto for me, and he is going to write another one. And I want to try to commission some more concertos from other composers I admire."

Wispelwey hasn't confined himself to repeating the Dvořák Concerto, the standard showpiece for cellists, over and over again; he has played concertos by Ibert, Schnittke, and Shostakovich as well as all the standard ones—his Elgar has been particularly admired. This season he is adding to his repertory the Bartók Concerto, originally written for viola.

Wispelwey speaks with precision and perception about his great predecessors. The name Gregor Piatigorsky comes up. "What I admire about him is that it was such honest cello playing—big, generous, but never tormented. This is the kind of music making I admire—no cheap schmaltz. He played like the old pianists. I guess when you are as tall as Piatigorsky, you feel safe in the world, feel safe to be happy. I do not so much admire the romantic, tormented cellists; I think a musician must be more like a chameleon. I think a musician should be more like Papageno in *The Magic Flute* than Sarastro."

Wispelwey expresses admiration for some of his contemporaries, particularly Ma ("the perfectionism"), Carr ("his emotion"), Ralph Kirshbaum ("such straightforward, juicy playing"), and Steven Isserlis ("what a splendid sound").

Nevertheless, throughout Wispelwey's career, his ideal musician has not been a cellist but a singer—Dietrich Fischer-Dieskau, who recently retired from singing, although he has begun to work again as a conductor. "All my life I have been collecting his recordings. In him, I find a superior balance between intelligent understanding and expressive interpretation. He is able to be immediate yet also able to keep a distance. To see him do Schubert's 'Winterreise' at the end of his career was extraordinary—here was a man in his sixties singing about the life of a much younger man. This experienced, elderly singer was so visionary, so suggestive; there was so much symbolism in his singing of every phrase. His singing was powerfully emotional yet very intelligent. In the simplest words he is able to find many layers of meaning. This I would like to be able to do on the cello."

Kermit Moore

4

SINCE THIS 1993 INTERVIEW, Kermit Moore has continued his multiple projects as cellist, composer, and conductor from his home base in New York City. In 1998, he soloed in music by photographer, composer, and poet Gordon Parks, playing with the National Symphony Orchestra under Leonard Slatkin. The performance appeared in a recent HBO documentary on Parks titled *Half Past Autumn,* and one of Moore's favorite recent projects was composing and conducting the music for a CD accompanying Parks' latest book of photography and poetry, *A Star for Noon.* In another recent project, Moore composed the music for a PBS documentary on Ralph Bunche (the first African-American division head in the Department of State and a 1950 Nobel Prize winner for his work with the United Nations in helping to broker disputes in the Middle East). Moore spends summers on the faculty of the Chamber Music Conference and Composers' Forum of the East at Bennington in Vermont.

MUSIC IN THE NEW WORLD

Edith Eisler

One of Kermit Moore's brochures bears the heading "Cellist—Conductor—Composer," another "Conductor—Cellist—Composer," and a third "Conductor—Composer—Cellist." His extraordinary musical versatility, which involves being at home in every style from Baroque to jazz, is based on a multiplicity of skills perfectly in keeping with his wide range of interests and intellectual pursuits. Moore is fluent in Latin and French, besides his native English, and he gets around in German and Italian. He spends a lot of time in libraries ferreting out unusual and neglected works for cello, and he has been a champion of contemporary music in general and American music in particular, as a player, conductor, and arranger. Describing a busy life divided into so many equal parts, he says, "I must be careful to keep track of what I'm doing and to practice the right pieces and study the right scores at the right time."

I met Kermit Moore in the late 1940s, when we were both studying at the Juilliard School of Music. I lost sight of him when he left New York and found him again when he returned in the early '60s. Over the years, I heard him in a number of recitals that I enjoyed and admired, but it was playing chamber music that really brought us together. It did not take me long to discover that, in addition to being a splendid cellist, he was a matchless partner, one of those rare people with the envious ability to bring out the best in their colleagues and enable them to play better than they think they can. He certainly had a liberating effect on me, through his unfailing responsiveness to the subtlest interplay, giving me a sense of constant support and reciprocity. I often told him that if there was anything I enjoyed more than listening to him, it was playing with him. Later, he invited me to play in several groups he was involved with, including the Symphony of the New World, the first orchestra in New York that actively welcomed minority players, which he had helped to found. I also knew him to be a fine teacher; both he and his wife, the composer Dorothy Rudd, joined the faculty of the newly founded Harlem School of the Arts soon after I did in the 1960s.

Kermit Moore was born in Akron, Ohio, where his musical life began at the age of five, when his mother started him on the piano. She also taught his older brother and sister.

What were your musical studies like at that age?

Being the youngest, I had to work hardest to catch up. At ten, I began to study the cello with Charles McBride, who had been a student of Willem Willeke in New York and played on the first stand of the Cleveland Orchestra. He was an excellent teacher; he realized that I loved the cello and would work hard. After a year or so of private study, he entered me in his class at the Cleveland Institute of Music, where I also took other subjects and played in the orchestra. All that was very good for me. After I left the Institute, I came to New York and studied with Felix Salmond at Juilliard, and that's when you and I met.

But didn't you go to college elsewhere?

Yes, I was going to New York University at the same time, studying musicology and composition.

Why didn't you study that at Juilliard?

They had a very good music department at NYU at the time: Marion Bauer, Curt Sachs; Philip James was head of the department and he actually was my composition advisor. You wouldn't call him a teacher, because he didn't believe you could teach composition; he would look at your work and pose problems for you. I studied a whole course of fugue writing with Dr. Gustave Reese. His first degree was in law, but he loved music and published a lot of books on it. Several of us graduate students helped him research one of them: we translated the neumes [notation used in early liturgical music] in Gregorian plainchant, and I also translated some Latin into English.

How long were you at Juilliard?

Three years. After I got my master's degree from NYU, I went to Hartford for three years, became principal cellist in the Hartford Symphony, and taught at the Hartt School of Music. We had a quartet in residence, which was very good; we traveled around the country and also made some records. That was a very important period for me, because I learned a lot from Béla Urban, the first violinist, who was much older than the rest of us. We had a very good relationship, and though we were all on the faculty, he was really a teacher for us. I also had the good fortune to act as a chauffeur to Raphael Bronstein [the eminent violinist and teacher], because we both commuted back to New York on the same evenings. I was 20 years old, and I would talk to him about whatever problems I had encountered in my teaching, so for a whole year, I virtually got a pedagogy course in my car.

And then?

I went to Europe. I wanted to study with Paul Bazelaire, who had been [cellist Pierre] Fournier's teacher, at the Paris Conservatoire. I went to him first at Fontainebleau for the summer; then I decided to stay with him and resigned from Hartford. At Fontainebleau I also began to study with Nadia Boulanger and worked with her for three years. She was the most intelligent person you can imagine. Both she and Bazelaire had an incredible super-intelligence. It's really wonderful to work with someone like that, because it's all gold and no dross.

In what language did you communicate?

With Bazelaire, in French; mine was good by then and of course improved every day. Boulanger prided herself on her English, and her Italian was also very good. I played in a concert she conducted with English, American, Italian and French musicians; we all knew French, but she used the three languages constantly in rehearsal to show how well she spoke them. Studying composition with her was important for me, because she made me more analytical and gave me more discipline than I'd had before.

Had you composed a lot by that time?

I'd written two string quartets that we had played in Hartford, a cello sonata, and a work for baritone and orchestra called

COMPOSITIONS

Kermit Moore's compositions are available for sale or rental from the Rud/Mor Corp., 33 Riverside Dr., New York, NY 10023.

Caraviaggio Revisited for Cello and Piano.

Five Songs for DRM (for soprano and piano, based on poems by Dorothy Rudd Moore).

Many Thousand Gone (for chorus, flute, string orchestra, and percussion).

Mombasa Ostinata for Strings.

Music for Cello and Piano.

Music for Flute and Piano.

continued...

Tetalestai. That's Greek for the last words of Christ, and it means "It is finished." That was the piece I brought to show her; as we worked on it, I totally rewrote it, and I learned a lot from that. She was also helpful to me in getting concerts and jobs.

Is that permitted in France? Don't they have labor laws?

Oh, technically, of course, I wasn't supposed to be working, but Boulanger cut some corners and some red tape, and I was never challenged. My first job in Paris was playing in René Leibowitz' orchestra. We recorded, among some other things, Schoenberg's *Gurre-Lieder.*

I have that recording!

We became very good friends; he was one of Schoenberg's last pupils. I also played in a little chamber orchestra conducted by the son of the Maréchal of Paris, and if he said it was OK, there wasn't likely to be any problem. [*Laughs.*]

I lived in Paris for three years, and then I moved to Brussels; I had played a recital there and had management in Holland. But I felt that Brussels was a better hub for getting around, and it was also less distracting than Paris: I could just be dull and practice. I met two wonderful people for whom I played every time I had to perform. They were both in their eighties. One was Emile Douhard, the original cellist of the Belgian Quartet, and the other was Amadé Vita. He had studied at the Brussels Conservatory with Edouard Jacobs, the man who refused to accept Casals as a pupil. Vita told me he witnessed that audition; the other students who were there laughed at Casals because he wore bad clothes, his hair looked strange, and every time he started a tempo, he got faster and faster. So Jacobs turned him down. I played for Casals in 1955, the last year he was in Prades [France]; I had a number of sessions with him. He was a wonderful person and a wonderful teacher.

During my four years in Brussels, I did a lot of research in the Library Museum, which is one of the best in the world for old works. There I came across a statement by Couperin: "On Sunday we gave concerts for the king. Alarius played the flute; I played the clavecin." And then I found a composition by Alarius. At that time, I was playing a lot of viola da gamba and formed a trio, with a flute and a harpsichord, which we called L'Ensemble Alarius.

Then, in 1961, I came back to America to play some concerts, but I wasn't planning to stay here. I don't really know why I decided not to live in Europe anymore, except that I visited my parents in Ohio and realized I didn't want to be so far away from them. And in 1964 I got married, and since then I've been playing concerts with several different managers all over the country.

But unfortunately you haven't played in New York recently.

No, and the reason is that if I give a concert here, I have to hire a hall, pay for it, and make all the arrangements myself. When I am engaged in other places, I get paid and all I have to do is play the concert.

Well, I miss hearing you, but you are busy enough playing all over the country.

Yes, playing and conducting.

Where did you study conducting?

Well, I had always conducted something, even as a teenager. Then, in New York, I was one of five people who played for Rudolf Thomas' conducting class at Columbia University, and in return he'd give us lessons. Later, in the 1950s, I spent three weeks auditing a master class with [Herbert] von Karajan in Milan, for which he used the Opera Orchestra. Auditors were allowed one problem or question, one moment in the limelight, when we could go up and conduct and have him demonstrate for us. So I had to choose my question carefully.

What was it?

The opening of Beethoven's Fifth Symphony, which, as you know, is notoriously difficult to make clear to an orchestra.

Did he answer it?

Oh yes, very well. He was meticulous; there was no waste in his language. But he was very patient with me; he probably gave me more time than he had to. He was never cold to any of us. I don't know if you'd call him friendly—open, perhaps. I got a lot out of it, even though I was only observing.

Tell me about some of the highlights of your conducting career.

I conducted in Europe before I got engagements here; after I had returned to America, I went back to conduct in Brussels, Switzerland, and Germany. Since then, I have done Schoenberg's *A Survivor from*

Warsaw with the Berkeley Symphony, twice—what a wonderful work!

There's a lot of Hebrew in it, and I felt I couldn't conduct a chorus without some knowledge of the language. So, taking it for granted that any of my Jewish friends would be able to help me with the text, I asked one of them to translate it for me and tell me how to pronounce it, and when he said, "I don't know a word of Hebrew," I felt so foolish!

However, he had a partner who not only knew Hebrew but was a survivor from Warsaw himself, and I thought, "Oh my God, this is too scary!" But he gave me the pronunciation, explained the principles, and helped me in all sorts of ways.

And then I talked with the conductor of the chorus on the telephone, and I said, "Now when we get to *this* passage, I want them to pronounce it like *that*." And he answered, "Yes, that's how I have also been advised." And we laughed, because obviously we'd both received help in the same way.

A couple of years ago, I conducted Duke Ellington's *Sacred Concerts* with the Brooklyn Philharmonic, at Avery Fisher Hall. The piece was written for voice, dance, and Ellington's band, and, at his family's request, I orchestrated it on a commission from the Cleveland Orchestra, which gave the first performance. Next year, I'm conducting it in Japan. In fact, I just got back from Japan, and it was nice to be able to make the arrangements personally.

What were you doing in Japan?

Playing with Ron Carter. You know, he's not only a great bass player, but also a very good composer. We played his pieces for four cellos and his own quintet. I've also recorded with him; a new album is out in Japan and is coming out here later.

Yes, I'm told that Ron Carter always relied on you heavily in recording sessions that required string sections. And he's not the only one: Judy Collins was quoted to the effect that whenever she walks into a studio and

COMPOSITIONS

(continued)

Music for Horn, Strings, and Percussion.

Music for Timpani and Orchestra (for timpani, multiple percussion, and full symphony orchestra).

Music for Two Violas and Piano.

Music for Viola, Piano, and Percussion.

Quincentra (for string quartet and piano).

Res Maximae (for percussion and strings).

Trois Tableaux (for cello and piano).

finds you there, she knows everything will be all right. Was it your recording career that introduced you to playing jazz?

Yes, when you make commercial recordings, you play everything and accompany everybody, from Leontyne Price to Lena Horne. From 1961, I worked regularly for ABC and CBS; some of the commercials and jingles I played are still being used. There were big names among my fellow cellists: George Ricci, Harvey Shapiro, David Soyer, Maurice Bialkin. I played with many jazz artists—McCoy Tyner, Sonny Stitt, Stanley Turrentine, Sir Roland Hanna—as well as the Bee Gees, Barbra Streisand, and of course Ron Carter and Judy Collins. I worked in the studios until 1988, but though I decided to stop at that point, I still do certain projects; for example, I recorded the sound track of *The Goodbye Girl*.

But you also record for a classical label, don't you?

Yes, it's called Performance Records. I've done the Brahms E-minor and the Mendelssohn D-Major Sonatas, the Mendelssohn *Song Without Words*, the *Fauré Elegy*, the *Ravel Chansons madécasse* with Hilda Harris, my own *Music for Cello and Piano*, and *From the Dark Tower* and *Dirge and Deliverance* by my wife, Dorothy. My regular pianist is Dr.

Raymond Jackson. These are all LPs; I hope to get some of them on CD soon [*Editor's note: As of this time these pieces are still unavailable on CD*]. I also recorded six string-quartet movements by Jerome Kern, with the faculty of the Bennington Conference (where I have been teaching for the last six summers). They are based on his own songs, and he arranged them himself with the help of Charles Miller; they are quite difficult and really good for the string quartet.

Didn't you also get involved in films at one time?

Yes, I've written several scores, one for a film called *The Ida B. Wells Story*, about a lady who was a newspaper publisher and philanthropist.

For another film, called *See You in the Morning*, I taught the actor Lukas Haas, who was then about ten years old, to play some cello exercises that I had composed and a bit of a Vivaldi concerto so it would look real on-screen. But of course, I played the sound track myself. I also co-composed with Gordon Parks the score to his film *Solomon Nothrup's Odyssey*.

Tell me about some of your more recent compositions.

Well, the latest is a string quartet with trap drums, written for Max Roach and the Uptown String Quartet in 1992. It's chamber music, not jazz—it just uses a jazz drum—but it's in a different vein from most of my works. There are a lot of harmonics in it, and I decided to leave nothing to chance—you know, so many composers are very vague about notating harmonics—so I wrote down where I want them played by using Roman numerals for the strings, and Arabic ones for the positions on the fingerboard. It makes my job a little harder, but it really works. It's called *Res Maximae*, as a pun on Max Roach's name.

Not his daughter Maxine's, the violist of the quartet?

Well, yes, that's also true. I wrote the piece on a commission from the Penfield Foundation in Rochester. In fact, I usually compose on commission, because otherwise I feel I'm robbing from something else.

There is a flute sonata written for Harold Jones, but it's also been played by many others. I have string quartets and a piano quartet commissioned by the University of Michigan; I wrote a piece for viola, percussion, and piano for Emanuel Vardi, and one for two violas and piano for him and his wife, who is also a violist. I've conducted the Detroit Symphony in *Many Thousand Gone* for chorus and orchestra, and I've also written a work for timpani and orchestra.

Do you ever play any chamber music in public now, your own or that of other composers?

No, it takes more time than anything else, and I simply don't have enough. So I haven't done that for many years, except at Bennington, and even there, though we know what we're going to play months in advance and have played together before, the six hours of rehearsal we set aside for a piece are never enough, and we often work deep into the night.

But I do have a rather big group called Classical Heritage Ensemble, in which I play; it was founded in 1985 for a symposium at the University of Michigan. We've played there and at other universities, also at the Brooklyn Academy of Music and Lincoln Center Out-of-Doors. We have enough people to perform Mozart symphonies, with me conducting, and we can split into small groups like string quartets, wind quintets, and so on. We premiered my piano quintet, which I wrote in 1991, at the University of Michigan. We also play for Hospital Audiences, Inc. There, the players get paid by ASCAP [American Society of Composers, Authors, and Publishers] on condition that at least one of my pieces appears on the program; I give my services without charge, for a good cause.

Another good cause in which you had a big role was the Symphony of the New World. I played in it for a while, but I've always wanted to know more about it.

It started in 1964; I was among its 12 founders and became the project director, principal cellist, and sometime conductor.

I remember—I used to call them the "Twelve Founding Fathers."

And mothers!

Yes! Who were some of the others?

Let's see—Benjamin Steinberg, who was also the first conductor; violists Alfred Brown and Selwart Clarke; oboist Harry Smyles, who was also the contractor; bassist Richard Davis; and percussionist Elaine Jones, who, in an inspired moment, came up with its name. We'd been sitting around trying to find one, getting very frustrated, when she said, "Why don't we call it the Symphony of the New World?" and we knew we had to look no further.

The purpose of the orchestra was to create performance op-portunities for all gifted young professional musicians, because we felt

that the makeup of symphony orchestras across the country was almost entirely white and male, despite the fact that there were many accomplished professional women, blacks, Hispanics, and Asians. It was a good idea; there was a need for an orchestra like that. Our aim was to help the young players get experience by having enough seasoned veterans to act as anchors, and that worked very well.

[Actor] Zero Mostel practically paid for our first concert at Carnegie Hall in 1965, and then we got money from other private sources, and from Exxon and the National Endowment and the [New York] State Council for the Arts, so a lot of people believed in us. And the orchestra was important in many ways; people got a great deal out of playing in it. Some learned a lot of literature, some got jobs they couldn't have got without it. We had some very good conductors and a wonderfully faithful audience.

Can you help me recall a few of those who later moved into major positions? I remember Noel Pointer, because of the lovely, sweet tone he got out of his violin; Jerome Ashby, the horn player who joined the New York Philharmonic . . .

As did two violinists, Marilyn Dubow and Myung-Hi Kim; another one, Booker Rowe, has been in the Philadelphia Orchestra for 20 years. Antoinette Handy, a flutist, is now head of the music division of the National Endowment for the Arts.

And Harold Jones, that other fine flutist, plays everywhere. How about the conductors?

After Steinberg left, Everett Lee became director. Guest conductors included James DePreist, George Byrd, Coleridge-Taylor Perkinson, Paul Freeman, Leon Thompson. For all of them, this was a good opportunity to conduct in a major hall. We also expanded the horizon of the New York audiences in terms of repertoire: we gave premieres of pieces like Beethoven's "Ne' giorni tuoi felice" for soprano, tenor, and orchestra, Dorothy's *From the Dark Tower,* and works by William Grant Still, George Walker, Ulysses Kay, Noel Da Costa. We put on concerts with celebrities from the jazz world, including Dizzy Gillespie, Yusef Lateef, and Duke Ellington.

Did you ever conduct any of your own works with the Symphony?

Yes, the premiere of *Many Thousand Gone,* in 1973.

To me, one of the most appealing things about that experience was the unusually warm, comradely atmosphere among the players; I thought that was remarkable in a group of people so diverse in age, sex, color, and

WHAT HE PLAYS

Kermit Moore's cello is a 1698 Francesco Ruggeri, formerly owned by the English cellist Anthony Pini. He also has a cello by Andrea Postacchini from 1826 and a Mittenwald cello from the early 1900s. He still has the gamba he used in Belgium, made in the early 1800s by an unknown maker, but he now uses it only for pleasure. His favorite bow is a Dominique Peccatte, and he also has two "reliable, friendly" Eugene Sartorys and a bow made by Sartory's son-in-law, Guy Dupuis. He uses Eudoxa C and G strings, and Jargar medium A and D strings.

nationality. Nobody seemed to care or even notice the differences. I always felt very much at home in it and was very sad when it disbanded—when was that?

After the 1975–76 season. It lasted about 12 years, and then it ran into financial difficulties, which unfortunately is not so rare among groups of this kind. But there was another premiere we did, of a piece that's very close to my heart: the Violin Concerto by Joseph White—did you play in that concert?

I don't think so. When was it?

In 1974. Ruggiero Ricci was the soloist; I conducted.

And who was Joseph White?

He was a Cuban composer who lived from 1837 to 1920. He succeeded [Delphin] Alard as professor of violin at the Paris Conservatoire. I had never heard of him, and when I found out who he was, I went in search of this violin concerto. The manuscript was found in Paris by Professor Paul Glass of Brooklyn College, and together we edited it and got it published in 1976. It then went out of print and has now been reprinted by Belwin-Mills. It's a wonderful piece; I conducted it again in 1990 with the Brooklyn Philharmonic and Winterton Garvey as soloist. Aaron Rosand has played it with the New York Philharmonic and also recorded it in London under Paul Freeman. This heads the list of my current interests.

Can you mention another one?

Well, I've been invited to speak to the subscribers of the New York Philharmonic on a lecture series called Music Plus, which precedes the Saturday concerts. I find this very stimulating, partly because it compels me to really study the scores. One lecture was on the new piece by [Olivier] Messiaen, which gave me a chance to attend the rehearsals with his widow, Yvonne Loriod, and my next one will be on Beethoven's Ninth Symphony. I've been asked to continue [this] season.

A full musical life of infinite variety—if that doesn't make a man a complete musician, I don't know what does.

I only know that I enjoy everything I do, and that's wonderful.

Hai-Ye Ni

5

AT THE TIME OF THIS 1997 INTERVIEW, Hai-Ye Ni was just beginning a promising career. She has since added Rio de Janeiro to the list of places she has toured, and the CD mentioned in the interview was released in the fall of 1997. She has performed with the Vienna Chamber Orchestra, at Lincoln Center, at the Pablo Casals Festival in Prades, France, and with Christoph Eschenbach, among her many engagements. She was also appointed associate principal cellist for the New York Philharmonic. She enjoyed playing the Vivaldi Double Concerto with Bobby McFerrin; he sang one cello part while she played the other. We have much to look forward to as this talented cellist continues to grow and to establish her place in the musical world.

ON THE THRESHOLD

John Lehmann-Haupt

As 24-year-old cellist Hai-Ye Ni sat poised for the opening Haydn trio in a recent concert at New York's Mannes College of Music, I jotted down the words "centered and strong." It was an impression of her manner, not her sound, but it was only enhanced by the supportive precision of her ensemble work, her warmly nuanced solo passages, and, when we later met, her reflections on her unfolding musical life. The story of her origins and development traces the emergence of a voice of substance and depth, and it's exciting to mark its arrival.

Born in Shanghai, China, in 1972, Ni emigrated in 1985 to study at the San Francisco Conservatory of Music. Honors soon followed, and in 1990 she became the youngest first-place winner in the history of the Naumburg Competition. With her recent first prize in the International Paulo Cello Competition in Helsinki and her 1996 Master's from Juilliard in hand, she is on the brink of a major career. In February she embarked on a 14-city U.S. tour to perform Bright Sheng's new concerto (following its premiere by Yo-Yo Ma, who commissioned it), and summer appearances at Spoleto and Ravinia are to come. Her debut CD is slated for release on the Naxos label this fall.

When Ni arrived at my apartment for our interview, she was friendly, direct, and inquisitively observant. As I fixed her a cup of tea, she flipped through some old LPs I had out, noting one by Mstislav Rostropovich with approval, and questioning me about a guitar transcription of a Bach cello suite on another. Although her English is not yet perfect, she speaks with care and precision.

"I started at the age of four, on the violin," she says. "My mother was my teacher; she's a cellist, but at that time it was very difficult to find a small cello in China. It's not like America, where you can rent one easily, because there aren't any shops except those belonging to the music schools, and we didn't know anyone there. So I began with the violin.

"At that time, it was the end of the Cultural Revolution and the country was not open to Western ideas. I didn't hear any live performances because there were none. But I listened to many old recordings. We had a big reel-to-reel machine at home and my mother would copy other people's records to play for me, so I heard Casals and [Pierre] Fournier and all the other great cellists. I remember hearing *The Flight of the Bumblebee* and also the famous short pieces that Casals had done.

"I also heard traditional Chinese music, mostly the opera, which they had on TV. But I think I followed more the story, the drama—how she died, how her husband avenged her, and so on. I was also interested in the costumes, with all the makeup and decoration. I listened more to classical music."

Ni says her formal training began when she was eight.

"I gave up the violin and started cello at the Shanghai Conservatory of Music. We had two private lessons a week, and we had to take a piano minor. We also had to practice a certain number of hours in school every day; there would be a person walking back and forth by the practice rooms to make sure everyone practiced. But any time I had a spare five minutes I would dash into the Ping-Pong room for a game!"

Although the relative isolation of Ni's beginnings might suggest that her early playing was unduly molded by the recordings she heard, it seems that from the start her sound was internally motivated.

"Basically it was something I felt within myself," she says. "It wasn't any particular type of voice I was looking for, but whatever felt the most natural to me. I was able to produce a very nice sound, a meaningful sound. The teachers and the public liked my playing, and I performed quite a bit for foreign visitors when they came to our school."

It was through a career opportunity for her father, at the time a professor of chemistry at the University of Nanking, that Ni found a bridge to the West that led to a crucial phase of her growth.

"In 1982, my father came to the States to do research on an exchange program at U.C. Berkeley. He had a cassette of my playing, and he gave it to [cellist] Margaret Rowell, who was a professor at the San Francisco Conservatory of Music. She was impressed with my playing—I think she liked my instinctive musicality—and she took the tape to the conservatory. Then in 1984, I toured the U.S. with a group of young dancers, singers, and classical musicians. When we got to San Francisco, she came to see me at the Consulate; I couldn't go out because it was an official tour. I played for her and she liked it very much.

"The next year my mother and I moved to Berkeley and I entered the preparatory school at the San Francisco Conservatory. I studied for seven years with Irene Sharp, a student of Margaret Rowell's, and she was very influential. When we first came, I was 13 and knew nothing of competitions or the business world of music. She suggested I go to regional competitions and gave me pieces to work on. Back in China, the emphasis had been more on the technical aspects of playing; one didn't get enough of the artistic side. Irene Sharp had me reading about music and composers, and going to many concerts."

One senses that for Ni there has been a series of awakenings to new knowledge and understanding that would have occurred quite differently had she been born in the West, where the appearance of such a talent would almost certainly have precipitated career aspirations much earlier on.

"Meeting Yo-Yo Ma was a big landmark," Ni comments. "He talked about things I had never thought about—where I wanted to be in five years, what kind of music I wanted to learn. I played the Kodály Solo Sonata for him in a master class when I was 15, and he asked me, 'Why do you want to do it this way, and not that way?' As a young person, I had always listened to my mother and then my teacher, who is like my second mother. But he said you have to think on your own, you have to explore.

"In a way Rostropovich was telling me the same thing, but I didn't know how to do it. For about two years we would go to Washington,

D.C., maybe twice a year, and I would play for him. I played the Schumann Concerto for him, and the Shostakovich Concerto No. 1. He could see that I could play very well and very musically but that I did most of it by instinct. He tried to open my eyes; each lesson was very intense. He's an extremely literary and cultured person, and he told me many things. Luckily I have a tape of one of the lessons. Now I can understand everything he's saying, but at the time, nine years ago, I was completely overwhelmed.

"When I finished at the conservatory in San Francisco, I went to Juilliard to study in the graduate program with Joel Krosnick, the cellist for the Juilliard Quartet. He had given a master class at the conservatory the year before, and the things that he said made so much sense to me, about how to see the phrase, all these structural things I was searching for. When I first played the Brahms F-Major Sonata, I realized I couldn't understand it with my natural instincts; it wasn't enough. When I had learned about theme and development in theory class, it was just dry information, but Mr. Krosnick helped me connect it all. He gave me a tool to learn a piece by myself."

Although Ni now has the analytical skills to match her natural gifts, her innate sensibility continues to guide her tastes and affinities. Her strong communicative instinct informs a perspective that encompasses old and new interpretive approaches alike. When I ask her how she perceived the contrast between the Romantic expressiveness of past generations and the crisper, perhaps more musicologically informed accents of many of today's players, her answer cuts to the heart of the matter.

"The trend of any art form is defined by individuals," she says. "Rostropovich's playing is so different from Casal's, but people love the beauty in it. So he became the icon, and everybody wants to copy him. Now Yo-Yo has come up, and they want to copy him. They're all great artists with a very strong message. I need to find what I think is artistic and beautiful—whatever makes sense to me—and then play that for people."

Ni's preferences in Bach interpretation reveal a similar breadth.

"[For Bach] I like Casals. It's like Shakespeare, where every time I go back—a year from now, five years from now—I always find something beautiful in his playing, something that attracts my attention to what he does with the phrasing. I also like Anner Bylsma. He's very different from Casals, a lighter kind of player. But his phrasings make a lot of sense to me; if I didn't know the piece, I would be able to understand it from his playing."

She speaks of Casals as a continuing inspiration.

"Just two days ago I took out a very old recording of his, that I had brought from China, with 12 short pieces by different composers—Bach, Beethoven, Haydn, Tartini, and others. He played everything so touchingly, so musically—it made so much sense, every single note. This kind of thing will never go out of style."

I was curious to know if Ni finds the same sort of beauty in contemporary music. At the Mannes concert, I had heard her perform in Bright Sheng's *Four Movements for Piano Trio,*

RECORDINGS

SCHUBERT: Sonata for Arpeggione in A minor, D 821; Mendelssohn: Sonata for Cello and Piano No. 2 in D Major, Op. 58; Beethoven: Variations for Cello and Piano on Mozart's "Bei Männern"; Schumann: *Phantasiestücke* for Clarinet and Piano, Op. 73; Popper: *Elfentanz,* Op. 39. With Hélène Jeanney, piano (Naxos 8554356).

which overlays pentatonic motifs reminiscent of Chinese folk music with chromaticism and sliding dissonances. But I wondered how she feels about more rigorous, less tonally oriented works.

"I've played the Henri Dutilleux Concerto," she responds, "which was written in 1970 for Rostropovich. It's maybe the most difficult concerto of the whole cello repertoire. It's not tonal music. But he has his own system; there's a fourth that he always uses. The way he combines different instruments to create certain moods—it's very beautiful. It's not traditional music, but it evokes the same kinds of feelings in you.

"Nowadays we have so much culture behind us, and we can do whatever we want. Many kinds of people are writing music—Chinese, French—and everybody is different, everyone has their own language. What I consider to be a good piece of modern music is anything that's coherent, interesting, and beautiful."

It dawns on me that all of Ni's observations are grounded in her own experience, never in supposition or the ideas or expectations of others. It is, I think, a key to her strength; there is about her an unassuming confidence that what is needed for her artistry will come in its own time.

"I haven't played that much recent repertoire yet, besides the Bright Sheng, the Dutilleux, and a few pieces by John Harbison," she continues. "I've premiered pieces in school for student composers,

WHAT SHE PLAYS

Hai-Ye Ni is, at the time of this interview, playing a Goffriller cello on loan from the San Francisco Conservatory for the Bright Sheng Concerto tour. (Like many young players, she has not yet been able to purchase an instrument commensurate with her artistry.) She uses a Jargar medium A string, a Jargar forte D, a Spirocore G, and a Spirocore tungsten C—a mix tailored specifically to the Goffriller, which she praises for "its warm, singing sound." Her bow is by the Paris-based American maker Robert Shallock; she admires its craftsmanship but would prefer it to have a little less give when she digs in. She uses a straight endpin, explaining, "Rostropovich uses the bent pin to his advantage; he's got such long arms. But it puts the instrument too far out for me."

mostly atonal and very difficult. But I do want to go forward with the cello. I can't yet know who the composers will be. I think I would play the Lutoslawski Concerto next, and there's a solo suite by Harbison based on a Bach suite, which I would like to look at. That's my plan for now."

She regards her career with a similar pragmatism.

"My career is just beginning," she says. "It would be so exciting to say, 'Oh, the Philadelphia Orchestra called and wants me to play.' I would definitely try to make it because a chance like that might not come next year. But I have to be especially careful that I do not do too much. I haven't traveled that much in comparison with Yo-Yo, but from the little I've done [Ni first toured following her 1990 Naumburg triumph], I've realized you do spend a lot of time on the road. There isn't much time to practice, and once you stop practicing, the playing goes down. What we do is a physical thing; we have to keep in shape."

It's perhaps not surprising that Ni speaks of performing with great enthusiasm—and as a form of communication that cannot be entirely planned in advance.

"[In performance] everything becomes alive," she says. "I feel much more free on stage than in a practice room, because it's like talking to someone. As a performer, the first thing I need to feel is the connection between me and the audience. I'm reacting to them, and everything becomes very different. It's a good sign when you discover something new on stage. If things are too much under control, you can do everything right but lose the spontaneity."

At the Mannes concert, I had been struck by Ni's seamless unisons with the left-hand piano line in the Haydn; they were a flawless blend of timbre, intonation, and rhythm.

"I think it can be harder to play the accompanying voice than the melody," she responds. "In Haydn quartets, you have to be the bass for the whole group, and if you don't know the structure of the piece, the harmonies and where the phrases go, you will go against the other lines rather than support them. A trio is different, because the cellist is more like a soloist. You have to be able to play the Dvořák Concerto to play the Brahms or Shostakovich Trio!"

Ni credits her three summers at Marlboro as a key influence in her exploration of chamber repertoire.

"My first group [at Marlboro] was with Felix Galimir, in the Brahms G-Major Viola Quintet. I also played the Berg *Lyric Suite* with him as second violinist, and Leila Josefowicz. That was a special experience. Mr. Galimir had premiered the Berg with his quartet, and he knew Schoenberg personally. He knows all this music by heart; he knows exactly who has what and what's going on. I also played with [pianists]

Don Weilerstein, Isidore Cohen, Barry Douglas, and Bruno Canino. It was a wonderful learning ground."

Ni has been compared in print to the young Yo-Yo Ma, although that is perhaps a journalist's facile device, for her sound is unmistakably her own. A signature characteristic of her playing, immediately noticeable in the Adagio from the Locatelli D-Major Sonata that opens her demo tape, is a dynamic pulse that not only shapes the phrases but also marks the rhythm in a way that is vibrantly warm.

"I think rhythm is the essence of everything," she says. "The way one speaks—every kind of emotion has a certain kind of rhythm."

In fact, every aspect of Ni's playing indicates that she is more than ready to meet what lies ahead. When I close with a standard interview question—When people in years ahead look back at you, as they now do at Casals and the others, what would you like them to say?—she answers with candor.

"I don't know if I have the courage to do what they did. It takes dedication, hard work, will, and courage. But I hope that for every concert, I will have given something to the audience, that I will have touched them in some way."

Ni may have her moments of doubt, and at this point, that is probably healthy. But, to invoke her own observation about the trend-defining potential of individuals, there are artists whose message has the power to make a mark. She may well be one.

Carlos Prieto

6

CELLIST CARLOS PRIETO HOLDS TWO degrees, speaks four languages, and is a tireless champion of Spanish and Latin composers. Since this interview in late 1997, he has continued to perform, write, and record at an astounding rate, and during the 1999–2000 season, he also hosted the first Carlos Prieto Latin American Cello Competition in Morelia, Mexico. His concerts often showcase a mix of Latin American and Spanish contemporary works as well as traditional works, and he continues to premiere important new pieces.

RENAISSANCE MAN

Edith Eisler

Carlos Prieto is a man of many talents. Born in Mexico City, he speaks fluent Spanish, English, French, and Russian. He holds degrees in engineering and economics from the Massachusetts Institute of Technology, and for several years he was the president of a metallurgical company in Mexico City. He is the author of several books, and, as if all this were not enough, he is also an acclaimed cellist who performs all over the world in prestigious concert halls and with great orchestras.

But perhaps his most remarkable achievement is creating a whole new cello repertoire through his untiring, dedicated championship of Spanish and Latin American composers. Since 1980, he has premiered more than 50 concertos, sonatas, and solo pieces. Most were written for him either on commission or as tokens of friendship and appreciation, and many of them he has also recorded.

Prieto took time to talk with me while visiting New York to play the complete unaccompanied Bach Suites in one evening at Alice Tully Hall. As he described his multifaceted career and wide-ranging interests, I constantly marveled at how anyone can learn and accomplish so much in one lifetime.

How did you come to play the cello?

There was a tradition of string quartets in my family. The first was formed by my grandfather, who played viola; my parents, who played violin; and an uncle who played cello. When I was born, this uncle no longer lived in the house and the quartet needed a cellist, so my mother bought me a cello the size of a violin. I began to study when I was three or four years old and immediately fell in love with the instrument.

My first teacher was Imre Hartman, the cellist of the Léner Quartet, Hungarians who had come to live in Mexico. Hartman was wonderful. I graduated from the Conservatory of Mexico when I was 16, having learned most of the big concertos, sonatas, and studies, and also having given recitals and played with orchestra. However, maybe unfortunately, I was also good in mathematics and physics, so, not being sure whether music was my vocation, I decided to apply to what I considered the most challenging university in the United States: MIT. I took two degrees there, and also became first cellist of the orchestra.

So I continued to play but not to study—though Boston is full of musicians—because I was pursuing two careers, and my first priority was to complete my courses in a satisfactory manner. But there was one distraction I could not resist: I spent many hours in MIT's very good music library, which contained a lot of Russian music. That's where I discovered Shostakovich. The library had all the recordings of his works available at the time, and I was immediately both impressed and shocked, because some of them struck me as magnificent, others as awful. I became so interested in Shostakovich and Russian music generally that I began to study Russian, and for two years took every course offered at MIT.

In addition to all of your other work?

Yes, and it bore good fruit. After I finished my studies, I returned to Mexico and worked for an iron- and steel-making company. Now, it so happened that a Soviet delegation came to Mexico, led by a very prominent politician named Mikoyan. They visited the plant, but the interpreter fell ill, so I was called in. Of course it's one thing to speak a language and quite another to act as interpreter, but I tried my best, and Mr. Mikoyan was much impressed that a young Mexican engineer should speak Russian and be so attracted to Russian things. I should make clear, however, that though I was interested in what happened in the Soviet Union and loved Russian music and literature, I never cared for its political system.

Mikoyan asked me if I would like to study in Russia. I said I'd love to go to the University of Moscow or Leningrad, but not to the University of Friendship of Peoples, because that was a political university. So, in my presence, he told the Russian ambassador to organize a visit for me. Time passed—six months, a year, two years. Finally, I received a telegram from the Soviet ambassador in Mexico City, saying, "Please come urgently to the embassy." Well, I was then working in Monterrey, 1,000 miles away, so I couldn't go urgently, but eventually I was told that I could spend a term at the University of Moscow.

This was in 1962, the years of Nikita
Krushchev, a very interesting period. People
were coming back from Siberia, [Alexander]
Solzhenitsyn was allowed to publish his first
book, many things were happening. One of
them was that Igor Stravinsky, a very close
friend of my family whom I had known all
my life, returned to the Soviet Union for the
first and only time. I could hardly believe it;
the Russian cultural authorities had written
the most awful things about him, and I knew
how he had reacted and that he hated the
system. But I went to his hotel, and he was
very kind to me and invited me to all his
rehearsals and concerts in Moscow.

A few months before this, Stravinsky had
been in Mexico to conduct and to attend the
opening of an exhibition of his wife's
paintings. One day he asked me whether
there were still bullfights in Mexico. I told
him there was one the next day, and he said,
"Please invite me—I love bullfights and I am
an expert." I'm sure not many people can say
they have been to a bullfight with Igor
Stravinsky, but I even have photographs to
prove it.

My Moscow stay was so interesting that I
started taking very careful notes, and they
became a book called *Russian Letters.* Many
years later, I started giving concerts in the
Soviet Union, which then consisted of 15
republics. I played in practically all of them,
from Siberia to the Caucasus, to the borders
of Afghanistan, Iran, China. . . . I was invited
every two years, so I had the opportunity to
observe the country in different political
periods, during the regimes of Krushchev,
Brezhnev, Andropov, Gorbachev, Yeltsin. My
last visit was in 1991, three weeks before the
end of the Soviet Union.

Ever since my first visit, I've always kept a
diary. After my last visit, someone at the
biggest publishing house in Mexico said to
me, "Why don't you organize everything

you've written down about your experiences in the Soviet Union?" And that became another book, *From the USSR to Russia.*

You must have been the only Western musician visiting Russia who did not need an interpreter.

Well, in any case, my Russian studies didn't go to waste!

After I returned from Moscow University, I eventually became head of the plant, then president of the company; I got married and soon had three children.

And did you still play the cello?

I always played the cello.

I assume you rescued your family quartet?

Of course! The second quartet consisted of my mother, who had taken over the viola, my father on first and my brother on second violin, and myself. Unfortunately, my parents died recently, but the quartet is continuing into the third generation with my brother as violist and my oldest son and oldest nephew as violinists. My son is a professional musician with a master's degree from Harvard University in business administration; he is now studying conducting and beginning to conduct in Mexico and elsewhere. My nephew studied economics, but two years ago he entered a national violin competition in Mexico and won first prize.

We rehearse whenever I am at home, and we also perform. Recently, we played three concerts in Mexico, including the festival in San Miguel. We play a lot of music, from Beethoven to Shostakovich, and we performed a quartet by my father's sister, Maria Teresa Prieto, who was a composer. So music is still in the family; the quartet, naturally, is called the Prieto String Quartet.

I am fascinated by this combination of so-called professionals and nonprofessionals. I'm sure the amateurs are very good, or you wouldn't play with them, and that you yourself also played very well when you were an engineer. I so often hear people say, "Why do I have to play accurately? I don't want to be a professional, I'm just doing this for myself." That makes no sense to me: one either plays well or badly, and always ultimately for oneself. You are living proof that the line between professional and amateur can be very thin.

That's true, but crossing it was still a very big step.

How did it happen for you?

Well, over time it had become ever clearer to me that I was a traitor to myself and to my real vocation, and I started making plans for severing all my connections with the Mexican industrial world. However, I had a position of responsibility: I was chairman of the Chamber of the Iron and Steel Industry of Mexico, and chairman of the Mexico-Japan and Mexico-Korea Business Committee, so you can imagine that it was not easy to make such a change. It took me three years to abandon everything and return to the cello.

My friends in the business world were saying, "Mr. Prieto has become insane. He is now devoting his life to the cello, but in less than a year he will recover his senses." And my friends in the music world were saying, "He will soon find out the difference between being a very good amateur and a professional; in a year he will go back to his former activities." Of course, I was fully aware that to be able to face the musical world, I would have to work terribly hard, but I was determined and confident that I could do it. Having studied 12 years when I was young and never really stopped playing, I had technique and repertoire to fall back on.

So I began to practice ten, 12 hours a day, and I studied with Pierre Fournier in Switzerland and Leonard Rose in New York on and off for several years. It was hard; I've often felt that if I had had a crystal ball to indicate the future and it had shown me exactly how difficult the transition would be, I might not have had the courage. But this is now 25 years ago and I've never regretted my decision. However, I must tell you that I developed an abiding obsession with recovering the time I lost from music. This has been a motor impelling me to do more and more—practicing, performing, studying. You know Proust's book, *Remembrance of Things Past?* It's part of a series called *In Search of Lost Time*. That's what I feel I am doing.

How did you start performing and establishing a career?

Of course the beginning was very difficult. The first thing was an invitation to join a group called Trio Mexico. The violinist was Manuel Suarez, the pianist his brother Jorge; I had known them for a long time, and they were very good. We toured around the world for three years.

In China, we were the first Western group to play chamber music, just at the end of the Cultural Revolution, in 1978. But by then, I was getting so many invitations as soloist that I had to leave the trio. We parted on very friendly terms. I gave the others all the time they needed to replace me, and the group still exists.

I started playing in Europe, especially Spain, and was lucky enough to get good reviews. My New York debut at Carnegie Hall in 1984 was also well received. When I played outside Mexico, I was sometimes asked to play a Mexican concerto, and to my great dismay I discovered that you could count the concertos written by Mexican composers on the fingers of one hand and still have several to spare. So I started trying to interest the most eminent among them in writing for the cello, such as Federico Ibarra, Manuel Enríquez, Blas Galindo, Joaquín Gutiérrez Heras, and Mario Lavista, as well as Max Lifschitz and Samuel Zyman, both Mexicans living in New York. That's how I got very much involved with contemporary music.

My obsession with recovering lost time also led to an obsession with recovering lost music, which took me to many libraries. Once I was told that Carlos Chavez, a prominent Mexican composer who died in 1978, had written a cello concerto, so I went to see his daughter— but she had never heard of it. I asked if I might look at his manuscripts, and in less than five minutes we discovered 100 pages, a first movement, of an unfinished concerto.

By now, I have premiered more than 50 works, and recorded many of them as well. Many of the pieces are dedicated to me, not only by Mexican but also by other Latin-American, Spanish, even some American composers: Celso Garrido-Lecca from Peru, Ricardo Lorenz from Venezuela, Gustavo Becerra from Chile, Roberto Sierra from Puerto Rico.

How do you find them?

Some of them I met when they came to Mexico or when I was on my tours. For example, when I played Strauss' *Don Quixote* with the San Antonio Orchestra a few years ago, the program included the premiere of a work by Robert Rodríguez, a very fine American composer, so he and I started planning a new piece. Some are well known: Astor Piazzolla and Alberto Ginastera from Argentina, Heitor Villa-Lobos from Brazil, Joaquín Rodrigo, who wrote the famous guitar concerto, from Spain.

There are many other Spanish composers not well known outside their own country: José Luis Turina, the grandson of Joaquín Turina, Manuel Castillo, Tomás Marco, and Roberto Gerhard, who emigrated to England during the Spanish Civil War. Leo Brouwer is a Cuban

living in Spain. Then there are two brothers, Ernesto and Rodolfo Halffter, who were on opposite sides in the civil war—Rodolfo went to Mexico, Ernesto stayed in Spain. Now a square in Madrid has been named after both of them.

Just before I came to New York, I did something that was very important to me: I played a three-concert cycle in Madrid called "Panorama of the Cello from Spain and Latin America in the 20th Century." The programs included works by most of these Spanish composers. Many of them were Spanish premieres.

When and how do you learn all this music?

By working incessantly. Next season, I am premiering at least six new pieces, including concertos by Carlos Farinas from Cuba, and Javier Alvarez and Marcela Rodríguez from Mexico. I am also writing a book about the history of all the composers with whom I have worked. There were many stories connected with the premieres, some funny, some not so funny, but above all I want to leave some kind of testimony for the future of how these pieces came to exist.

When do you find time to write your books?

On airplanes—that's where I have nothing to do, so I study scores and write books. My second one was called *Around the World with a Cello.*

Amazing! So you came here from your Spanish marathon for a Bach marathon.

This is the second time I've played the Bach Suites at Lincoln Center.

You play them in chronological order?

Yes. They get more complicated both technically and musically, and I think that must have been Bach's intention.

Isn't it very strenuous to play the two most demanding suites at the end?

Let me tell you a story to prove my endurance. Between the cycle in Madrid and the trip to New York, I played the complete Suites in several cities in Mexico. In Tampico, I arrived at 7 A.M. and was told that, in addition to the concert that evening, I was to play the Suites for the students of the university's music school that morning. So I played them twice that day, six times in five consecutive days. But I enjoyed it; it's all part of my obsession with making up for lost time.

How much time do you feel you lost?

About ten years. But of course they were not really lost. For example, my background in engineering and economics enabled me to write about Russia and the changes there from a much broader point of view

WHAT HE PLAYS

Talking with Carlos Prieto about his cello opens a whole treasure trove of fascinating instrument lore. For about 20 years, he has played on the famous "Piatti" Stradivari, made in 1720. "In the Hill book about Antonio Stradivari [*Antonio Stradivari: His Life and Work*]," he explains, "it is first mentioned as being bought in 1818 in Cádiz, Spain, by an Irish wine merchant, who took it to Dublin, then sold it in England; eventually the great cellist Alfredo Piatti acquired it.

"After my concerts in Madrid, I went to Cádiz to find out more about its origin. Unfortunately, I did not succeed, but the people there got very interested and invited me to perform the Bach Suites next year. This will be the first time the cello is played in Cádiz since it left there almost 180 years earlier." As to how it got to Cádiz, Prieto says, "At that time there were more than 50 Strads in Spain, including eight or nine cellos. Only two are left, and they are in the collection of the Royal Palace, which has a quartet of decorated Strads, plus a second cello. These instruments, all inlaid, were made by Stradivari before 1700, expressly for the king of Spain.

"Cremona was in the Duchy of Milano, which belonged to the Spanish crown. King Philip V went to Cremona in 1702 and Stradivari wanted to present him with these instruments, but the Cremonese authorities would not allow it because Spain was engaged in a war of succession. Then around 1775, King Charles III, who probably knew about these instruments, sent a priest to Cremona with the mission of buying them.

"I was invited to hear them at the Palace and to play the cellos. They are kept in a special vault and were brought out by Palace guards in very elegant uniforms. The cellos are in such heavy cases that each requires two guards to carry it, so seven guards appeared with five instruments.

"The reason there were so many Strads in Spain is that the country was musically very active, especially Cádiz, Madrid, and Barcelona, and it had a close connection with Italy. Many Italian musicians lived in Spain, such as than if my books had just been about music. I was very fortunate to be able to attend MIT, which is not only a fine school but also such an exciting place, full of wonderful musicians. And recently, I was appointed member of its Department of Music and Theater Arts Visiting Committee. That made me very happy.

Scarlatti and Boccherini—himself a great cellist who played on a great Strad. Besides, there was much music at the court, and King Charles IV, whose father had bought the instruments, was fond of playing the violin. He was a very mediocre king and, I imagine, an equally poor violinist, but he liked playing second fiddle in string quartets; the first violinist was a Frenchman named Alexandre Bouché. Whenever the King had several bars' rest, he would get confused and come in too early, so Bouché told him: 'Your Majesty, you must learn how to wait!' Charles, not accustomed to being addressed in this manner, retorted, 'The King of Spain waits for no one!'

"Another time, he criticized his part in a new quartet by Boccherini so harshly that the composer, who had a temper, exploded, 'Your Majesty, you should learn something about music before expressing such an opinion!' Charles, who had a worse temper, took him by the neck and threw him out."

I asked Prieto how he got his cello. "From the Marlboro Foundation [in Vermont]," he said. "It was used very infrequently, so Rudolf Serkin decided to sell it. My friend Jacques Français, the [New York] violin dealer, told me Serkin had stipulated that the cello be sold to someone who would play it a lot, so I said I was planning about 106 concerts for the next season. That satisfied Mr. Serkin. In my book about the Spanish and Latin-American composers, there will be a chapter on my cello and my experiences with it."

Prieto's strings are a Jargar A, Helicore D, and Thomastik G and C. About his bow he said, "For years, I played with a Peccatte. But when I studied with Leonard Rose, he once gave me a bow to try; I didn't know what it was, but I fell in love with it. Rose introduced me to the maker, William Salchow in New York, who made one for me, and since then, I've been unable to play with any other bow. Yesterday, Salchow said to me, 'Your program for the Bach says you will be performing on the "Piatti" Strad; it should also mention that you'll be using a Salchow bow!' He's right—it's a terrible omission."

Jian Wang

7

THE YOUNG CELLIST JIAN WANG is enjoying a career that is growing and maturing at a dizzying pace. Yet, as this interview from late 2000 reveals, his approach to his rising stardom is understated, even humble. Wang began his musical education in his native China and continued it in the United States, aided in his move to the West by musical mentors including violinist Isaac Stern and cellist Aldo Parisot. He soon began touring internationally in performances with such groups as the Detroit Symphony under Neeme Järvi, with the Tonhalle Orchestra in Zurich, and Amsterdam's Royal Concertgebouw under Riccardo Chailly. As a chamber player he has performed with pianist Yefim Bronfman and violinists Isaac Stern, Cho-Liang Lin, Maxim Vengerov, and many others.

AN EXTRAORDINARY JOURNEY

Andrew Palmer

When violinist Isaac Stern visited China in June 1979, he was among the first Western musicians granted access to the country as it emerged from the Cultural Revolution. A few years earlier he would have been demonized as a representative of the imperialist West; now he was welcomed for bringing a breath of fresh artistic air to a country that had spent 13 years rejecting any foreign influence on its culture.

His visit was documented in the 1981 Academy Award–winning film *From Mao to Mozart*. The last 15 minutes of the film show a ten-year-old pupil at the Shanghai Conservatory earnestly playing his cello before the distinguished foreign visitor. Twenty years later, Stern describes that cellist as "one of the finest young instrumentalists of our time." This is the story of his extraordinary journey from a closed society to an international career on the concert platform.

Sitting opposite Jian Wang in his small, neat apartment on the South Bank of the River Thames in London, I reflect on the fact that many famous instrumentalists share something in addition to talent and musicality: they were born into countries governed by oppressive political regimes, from which music was their means of escape. Could this explain why so many distinguished soloists have emerged from the East?

"That's a very good analysis," Wang replies. "In England or the United States, youngsters can do so many things because they have so many choices. But I was born in a country where life was difficult, where music was one of the few things you could study. When people leave China to study somewhere, they don't back off or say, 'I don't feel like doing this any more; it's becoming too difficult,' because usually that's not an option. We *have* to succeed. So I think you can say that the disadvantages of being born in a country where life is difficult become an advantage. We're driven because we have no choice."

Wang was set a powerful precedent by his father, who comes from a landowning family that lost most of its assets when the Communist Party came to power. Refusing to become a peasant farmer, he ran away at the age of 15 to the city of Xian (home of the famous Terracotta Warrior statues) and found work there. One day, while walking through a square, he heard Chinese music being played by a symphony orchestra and was spellbound. Deciding that music was to be his life, but having no one to teach him, he set about educating himself.

Wang's father bought an er-hu, the traditional Chinese two-stringed violin, and eventually enrolled at the Shanghai Conservatory, where he studied the cello. He also met a flutist, whom he married after they both graduated. However, as Jian explains, the prospects for talented young musicians in China were very limited. "During that time, the height of the Cultural Revolution, all Western music was banned except for a strange phenomenon called the Model Plays, which could be described as a mixture of Chinese opera and Western musical theater. The music, by Chinese composers, was set to stories by Communist ideologues that described the life of soldiers, peasants, and government officials. They used a full-sized Western orchestra with some Chinese instruments in it.

"In those days, too, the government decided where you worked when you graduated. Because my father was one of the best players in the conservatory, he was assigned to a Model Play company in Shanghai. Naturally, my mother wanted to stay with him. But she was given a job teaching in a school near Xian, so she couldn't. She applied for permission to join him, but this was refused. And in the meantime I was born.

"When I was three years old, my parents decided that life in Shanghai would be better for me—it was the richest city in the country, and if you could get in you'd have a much brighter future. So I went to live with my father, while my mother continued to apply to join us." (It was not until nine years later that permission was granted and the family was permanently reunited.)

The move to Shanghai marked the beginning of a plan to cultivate music in the young child and thus to equip him for as full a life as possible. While Jian was still an infant, his father gave him a violin with a stick planted in its end to form a makeshift miniature cello, simply to see what the child could do with it. The results were immediate and encouraging—he could in fact do quite a lot—and serious tuition began soon afterwards.

It is easy to imagine the frustration Wang's father must have felt during this period: a promising musical career redirected, if not curtailed, by the authorities; separation from his wife; and sole responsibility for bringing up their only child. Little wonder that, recognizing his son's instinctive gift for music, he threw himself into training the boy. Perhaps *he* might one day enjoy the freedom denied his father. But how did such an ambitious plan become a reality?

"Now that I'm famous in China," says Wang, "everyone wants to know what happened. In fact, a Chinese publisher wanted my father to write about how I grew up. For a long while he refused, but eventually he wrote something and it was published in a newspaper. When I read it I was amazed, and very touched, because I'd always thought all those ideas I had about playing came from my own head. In fact they came from him. But because he made me feel that *I* had come up with them, I was always very confident. That's why he was such a good teacher."

There remained a major hurdle, however: entry to the Shanghai Conservatory, where young Wang could have the type of schooling

necessary for a musical career. More than ever before, music was being seen as an escape route from conscription or forced labor in rural China. (Many people who were sent to live and work on peasant farms never returned, Wang explains sadly.) At the same time, restrictions on learning Western music were gradually being lifted. As a result, the conservatory was inundated with applicants. Fortunately, Wang met the strict entry requirements, for at the age of nine he was already an accomplished instrumentalist and had perfect pitch.

"I'd like to think that we received a full education there," he reveals, "but the truth is that we did not! They taught us mathematics, basic physics, and history, which was linked very closely to Chinese politics. But the rest was music: solfège, theory, and composition. We'd practice in the morning and have classes in the afternoon, or vice versa; practice sessions were 45 minutes each, and teachers would circle around to make sure we weren't being lazy. It was extremely regimented."

Wang's father negotiated a special arrangement with the teachers at the conservatory. Lacking the right kind of papers to be his son's "official" cello teacher, he was nevertheless recognized as holding the key to the extraordinary progress of their star pupil, and he was allowed to come in each day to coach him.

It was at this point that Isaac Stern entered the picture and, through the film of his visit to Shanghai, brought Jian Wang to the attention of the West. In a way, Wang recalls, Stern caused his own cultural revolution among the pupils at the conservatory. "China was so closed up, and everybody was rigid and afraid. There were a lot of talented musicians in the school, but the general feeling among them was 'better to be right and boring than interesting and wrong.' Mr. Stern changed all that. He was funny, he was sarcastic, he spoke in metaphors. And he did things with the violin that made the students love him.

"I was ten years old at the time," Wang continues, "and not sophisticated enough to understand everything he said. But when I saw him playing his instrument I just had a gut feeling that *this* was what you're supposed to do on stage. *This* was what you're supposed to give an audience. Before then, the feeling had been simply, 'I have to play all the notes correctly and get the intonation right.'"

Wang points out that in his early days at the conservatory, many on the teaching staff wanted to change the way he played because it was "incorrect." His father resisted this, believing that if something worked, it shouldn't be changed. Fortunately, the president of the con-servatory agreed. "It was the funniest thing when Isaac Stern visited us," Wang recalls, "because everybody whispered, 'How can he play the violin like that? He does it completely the wrong way!' Of course, when Isaac Stern plays as well as that, and it's the 'wrong' way, what can you say about it?"

Wang maintains that he was a slow learner, largely because of his father's philosophy of teaching. It was a step-by-step approach that built solid foundations through playing scales, exercises, and passages rather than "stretching" the technique with difficult works. Later, when Wang was given small, complete pieces, the emphasis was on playing them as musically as possible. A mature but naturally cautious child, he accepted this method and was unimpressed by the outwardly showy efforts

SELECTED RECORDINGS

Some of these titles can be difficult to find in the U.S. but can be ordered from international Web sites such as the Crotchet Classical Web Store (www.crotchet.co.uk).

BRAHMS: Piano Trio No. 1 in B Major, Op. 8; Piano Trio No. 2 in C Major, Op. 87. With Augustin Dumay, violin; Maria João Pires, piano (Deutsche Grammophon 447 055-2).

HAYDN: Cello Concerto in C Major, Hob. VIIb:1, Cello Concerto in D Major, Hob. VIIb:2. Gulbenkian Orchestra, Muhai Tang, cond. (Deutsche Grammophon 463 180-2).

continued...

of his classmates when they performed technically demanding works. "To be honest," he remembers, "I listened to them playing all these concertos—often so badly—and said to myself, 'I don't want to do that. I'd rather do something simpler.' I was so serious! But that's my personality, I guess. And I've never had big ambitions. Actually, when I was 16, all I could play was the Haydn C-Major Concerto, the Saint-Saëns No. 1, the Tchaikovsky *Rococo Variations,* and one movement of the Dvořák Concerto. Apart from a lot of small pieces, that was it."

Stern now confirms the value of this softly-softly approach. "Jian has the ability, given to very few young people, to, as the French say, 'live well in his own skin.' In other words, he doesn't bedevil himself with false hopes and great wishes that may or may not be attainable. This means that he attains, *happily,* things he doesn't expect.

"His greatest gift is his utterly natural and profoundly good musical instinct. He understands the inexplicable connections within a musical line because he *sings* naturally on his instrument. And that's the most important attribute in a musician. What I'm telling you about are mature attributes that one discerns later on, but what one could hear even then was his original instinct for music."

In 1982, at the age of 13, Wang left China for the first time and toured the United States in one of two music groups from the Shanghai Conservatory. Quite apart from the pace of work (his trio gave 57 concerts in 60 days), the culture shock was enormous. Disneyland, the addictive qualities of Coca-Cola, and the sense of freedom—being able to get into a car and drive anywhere, or board a plane or train freely—overwhelmed him. Less positively, he was surprised by the immaturity of American schoolchildren. "The 13-year-olds, and even some 15-year-olds, behaved like nine-year-old Chinese people, and this shocked me a little bit. They really had no idea what they were talking about!"

Back home in China after the tour ended, Wang had no way of knowing that he would return to the U.S. for a much longer period, thanks to another individual, as influential in his future career (albeit in a different way) as his father had been. Sau-Wing Lam, a music enthusiast who had left China in 1948 and built up a large and prosperous business in the U.S., saw *From Mao to Mozart* and was fascinated by the young cellist. Through the director of the Shanghai Conservatory, an old schoolmate, he made inquiries about the boy and learned of his exceptional promise. Lam then wrote to China's Minister of Culture, proposing to help Wang further his studies in America. The door was slammed in his face. China was proud of its budding cellist, he was told, and saw no reason to send him abroad to complete his training.

By 1985, however, Wang had become frustrated with life at the conservatory. Needing to accomplish more in his playing, but realizing that none of his teachers could tell him how, he was losing motivation to continue. There were occasional visits from foreign musicians that lifted his spirits, but they were not enough. Lacking inspiration, he was being starved musically.

By this point the political situation in China had relaxed somewhat, and Lam wrote to Wang's father, offering financial assistance to secure the boy's future. "This guy wasn't related to us, and we'd never met him," Wang says, "but he said he would sponsor me. I could choose any school I wanted, and he would pay for everything. He would give me a cello and money to live on. He promised my father (I still have the letter he wrote): 'I will treat him as if he were my own son.' It was unbelievable.

"When I explained that I wanted to study with Aldo Parisot at Yale, because I really loved the way he taught when he visited Shanghai, Mr. Lam said, 'No problem.' He contacted the school, deposited money for my fees, picked me up from the airport, and took me to his home. Then he drove me to Yale for my first lesson. He was a remarkable man."

Wang's studies while at Yale included technique—he admits that only within the last five years has he been able to achieve everything he wants to technically—and interpretation, including color and dynamics. One of Parisot's main tasks was to free him to be more expressive in his playing, for some of the rigidity of his Chinese training still remained. However, Wang emphasizes that he is essentially an introverted performer. "If I had the choice between playing as if I were coming out and hitting you over the head with a big club to impress you, or sitting there quietly as if to say, 'Maybe you'd like to hear this story . . . ,' I'd go for the latter. But of course Mr. Parisot taught me well, so I *could* come out and hit you over the head if I wanted to."

The teacher was alternately intrigued and exasperated by his new student. Wang's father's method had been thorough and effective, but it arguably left the teenager overconfident in his own judgment. It had certainly not opened him to the suggestions

SELECTED RECORDINGS

(continued)

MESSIAEN: *Quartet for the End of Time.* With Gil Shaham, Myung-Whun Chung, violins; Paul Meyer, clarinet (Deutsche Grammophon 469 052-2).

MOZART: Piano Trios K. 496 and K. 502. With Augustin Dumay, violin; Maria João Pires, piano (Deutsche Grammophon 449 208-2).

PRESENTING JIAN WANG. Works by Chopin, Barber, Schumann. With Carol Rosenberger, piano (Delos 3097).

SCHUMANN: Piano Quintet in E-Flat Major, Op. 44. With Maria João Pires, piano; Augustin Dumay, Renaud Capuçon, violins; Gérard Caussé, viola (Deutsche Grammophon 463 179-2).

of others, and when Parisot asked him to do certain things with which he disagreed, he usually refused. Eventually a compromise was reached. "He's such a wonderful teacher," Wang explains, laughing at the memory of his own stubbornness, "and he'd say to me, 'Okay, if you don't want to do this, then you must show me how you can do it differently.' So I'd do it my way. Sometimes I succeeded, but mostly I didn't.

"It took me a long time, but eventually I began to think. I remembered everything he told me, and decided that if my way didn't work, I'd always try his. And I'd always do it well. That's why he liked me. He used to say, 'It's difficult to get you to do something my way, but once you do it, it's always very, very good!'

"However, I'm still afraid of doing something I don't believe in. If I did everything on stage that I liked and felt was good, and the public didn't like it, I'd be upset, but I could live with that. However, if I went up there and did something I didn't believe in, simply because my teacher had told me to do it, I'd feel terrible because it wouldn't be *me* that the public disliked. I've never wanted to do anything that is not mine."

Unlike many prodigies, Wang first encountered much of the cello repertoire as a teenager rather than as a young child. When I ask if there were works that made a particular impression on him, he replies without hesitation, "The Shostakovich Concerto No. 1. I have a tape somewhere of [Mstislav] Rostropovich giving the U.S. premiere of the work and playing like a god. I remember that when I first heard it, I told myself half-jokingly, 'I'm going to stop! It's impossible—nobody can play the cello like that!' I was so impressed by the Concerto—and by Rostropovich, of course. He's definitely the cellist that I respond to."

After three years at Yale, Wang moved to New York to continue his studies at the Juilliard School. Still supported by the family of Sau-Wing Lam, who died in 1988, he enrolled for a bachelor's degree but was gently kicked out after three years because he was giving too many concerts to attend classes. By this time the qualities of his playing—the precise intonation, the throbbing intensity of his vibrato, and the ability to draw long, lyrical phrases from his instrument—were obvious. While based in New York, another fortuitous bolt arrived from the blue when he formed an unexpected musical partnership with violinist Augustin Dumay and pianist Maria João Pires. Thanks to the persistence of Wang's French manager, the duo had eventually agreed to play a single movement of a piano trio with him while they were all in France for the Montpellier Festival. None of them, it seems, was prepared for what happened next.

"During the rehearsal it was as if I could feel everything they were doing, and could respond to them," Wang remembers. "And when I did things, *they* would respond. I couldn't believe it. Really, we sounded as good together as we do on our recordings! I could tell they were very happy. Later on Augustin came to me and said, 'We've enjoyed playing with you so much. We'd like to form a permanent trio with you, to record for Deutsche Grammophon and to play this concert and this and that. . . . ' My jaw dropped open. It was a fairy-tale meeting."

Their first recording, of Brahms' Piano Trios Nos. 1 and 2, was released in 1996. "In Jian Wang," wrote *Gramophone*'s critic, "the duo

of Augustin Dumay and Maria João Pires have found themselves a true soul mate."

After leaving Juilliard, Wang settled in Europe. For a while he lived in Portugal, and then in Paris, but now he has made London his home, for personal and professional reasons: his Portuguese girlfriend is studying at Oxford, and—as both a performer and an audience member—he thrives on the bustle of the musical scene in the English capital. And then there is his growing discography. In 1990 he made a now-forgotten debut recital CD (with pianist Carol Rosenberger) for Delos; ten years on, he is an established Deutsche Grammophon artist.

WHAT HE PLAYS

Jian Wang plays a very old instrument: the Antonio and Girolamo Amati of 1622. The last musician to use it regularly was Daniel Heifetz, principal cellist of the NBC Orchestra. Wang remembers watching an old film of Arturo Toscanini conducting the orchestra and suddenly seeing his cello on the screen. "Did I recognize it immediately, by sight? Of course. It's a beautiful instrument."

He first played it in 1985, the year he left China. "By the time Sau-Wing Lam sponsored me to go to the United States, the cello was in his collection," he explains. "I started by borrowing it when I had important concerts to play, but I would always give it back afterward. He told me I could keep it, but I wasn't happy to do this while I was still a student. So he bought me a different one, a German instrument.

"In 1992, four years after he died, I started to play a lot of big concerts, and his widow and family decided that they would loan the Amati to me long-term. So I've had it for about eight years now."

His bow is the famous F.N. Voirin once owned by Emanuel Feuermann. "It's also in the film—I saw Feuermann using my bow!" he declares. "His cello was sold to my teacher, Aldo Parisot, together with the bow, and I acquired it from him.

"I'm not very picky about strings, and I tend to play whatever I've got. When I hear about a string that's supposed to be very good, I buy one, but I don't usually use it because I'm too lazy to change it! And if one breaks, I just put something on and keep it, unless I really hate it. However, for G and C I do like Thomastik Spirocores, because they're thinner and more responsive. And I like Larsen strings for A and D."

His recording of the Haydn cello concertos was released early in 2000, followed by the Schumann Piano Quintet (with Pires, Dumay, Caussé, and violinist Renaud Capuçon). Later that year he gave a number of performances of the Brahms Double Concerto in the U.S. with Gil Shaham—an old friend, orchestral colleague, and chess partner; they will record the concerto when they, and conductor Claudio Abbado, can find a mutually convenient date. "I'm also supposed to record all the Beethoven cello sonatas with Miss Pires," he says, "but you never know with her. I'm ready any time she is, though!" Meanwhile, D.G.'s recent release of Messiaen's *Quatuor pour la fin du temps*, in which Wang is partnered by Shaham, Paul Meyer, and Myung-Whun Chung, is gathering mixed reviews, its deficits doubtless a reflection of the time constraints in preparing and recording a CD these days.

Poised on the threshold of a major international career, Jian Wang retains great personal warmth and charm, displaying as much humility away from the limelight as he does authority and dynamism when in it. "He's an adorable human being," Isaac Stern confirms. "Everywhere he goes, he elicits two things. One is an affectionate embrace from everybody who's met him, and the other is a return engagement. That's the clearest sign of his talent." Wang seems genuinely grateful for his success, and one senses in him an awareness that his life could have turned out very differently indeed—as it must have done for many of his compatriots.

How, I ask, would he summarize the influence of his Chinese background on his playing of Western music? "It's funny," he smiles, "because when I'm in China I feel more American than anything. When I'm in America I feel more European. And when I'm in Europe I feel Chinese! It's very complicated. But let me answer your question this way.

"Chinese people are very moved to see somebody who has a difficult life but keeps a smile on his face. That touches us much more than somebody who's suffering but complaining about it to everybody. So I'd say that I prefer to speak to people through music in a very quiet way. Western culture is a bit more dramatic—look at paintings, for example. In the West, they're full of color and drama and battles, and they always show people. The majority of Chinese paintings are watercolors, and most of them are black and white. And they're about nature, not people. For me, that's the difference."

Ralph Kirshbaum

8

RALPH KIRSHBAUM'S CAREER AS A CELLIST is as remarkable for its breadth as its depth. Literally since childhood, he has been a teacher as well as a player, and now, as an established performer, his interest in pedagogy has only increased. He founded and continues to run both a festival and an award for young cellists, while also maintaining a busy international career as a soloist, chamber musician, and recording artist. As this 1998 interview reveals, he combines musical intelligence and professionalism with warmth, charm, and an infectious love of the cello and its repertoire.

CHAMPIONING THE CELLO

Edith Eisler

C omposers are writing so much more for cello these days that our repertoire has expanded beyond recognition in the last 30 years," says cellist Ralph Kirshbaum happily. And he has been in the forefront of those who have been spreading enthusiasm for the instrument and its literature.

Kirshbaum is a man of multiple accomplishments, and his wide-ranging interests keep him active in many capacities. A renowned performer, he appears all over the world in summer festivals and recitals, with major orchestras, and in chamber music with colleagues such as violinists György Pauk and Robert McDuffie, and pianists Peter Frankl and Misha Dichter. His discography ranges from Baroque to contemporary, including Bach's unaccompanied Suites, concertos by Haydn, Elgar, and Walton, and the Triple Concertos of Beethoven and Michael Tippett. Born in Texas, he makes his home in London but visits his native country four or five times a year.

A dedicated teacher, Kirshbaum has been on the faculty of the Royal Northern College of Music (RNCM) in Manchester, England, since 1976 and is much in demand as artist-teacher in workshops and master classes, including Isaac Stern's regular Carnegie Hall Chamber Music Workshops for Young Ensembles. In 1987, he established the Pierre Fournier Award, which gives a London debut recital to a deserving young cellist, and a year later he founded the Manchester International Cello Festival, held at RNCM in alternate years, which attracts many renowned cellists and hundreds of music lovers from around the world. Although there is no direct link between the Fournier Award and the festival, they are strongly connected by Kirshbaum's commitment to help aspiring young cellists develop their talents and further their careers.

The festival's international character reflects Kirshbaum's own background. "I grew up in Tyler, a small town in Texas," he tells me during a visit to New York in March 1998, and he laughs when I ask how a family named Kirshbaum had chanced to settle there. "My grandfather, whose name was Kirschenbaum (German for *cherry tree*), was a tailor in Czarist Russia," he explains. "He was taken prisoner by the Japanese in the Russian-Japanese war, and when he was liberated, he went to California, where he married an Austrian immigrant to America. My father was the result of that union; he became a musician and wanted above all things to conduct, so he went where conducting would be an integral part of the job. After many moves we eventually settled in Tyler, Texas."

Kirshbaum's musical training started at home, and formal study began with Lev Aronson, himself a pupil of Gregor Piatigorsky and the principal cellist at the Dallas Symphony for 25 years (he also taught cellists Lynn Harrell and John Sharp). Kirshbaum continued his studies with Aldo Parisot at Yale University, where he graduated with highest honors. "Then," Kirshbaum says, "I got a grant from the French government to study in Paris for a year. But it wasn't a happy experience—my teacher [Kirshbaum discreetly won't mention the name], who was very famous and did wonderful things for a whole generation of cellists, just wasn't right for me at that time in my life. It's the sort of thing that can happen to anybody. So I only had a few lessons and then simply stopped.

"But I stayed in Paris because I was learning a great deal in other ways. I played chamber music every weekend with very fine musicians, like [violinist] Salvatore Accardo; we'd get together for a whole day and play string quartets. I'd never had that kind of experience before, and it was fantastic. So when the year of my grant was up, I went to the director of the program and asked for an extension. That took courage, or should I say chutzpah, because I had to confess that I wasn't taking lessons anymore. But I convinced her that being in Paris was so valuable for me that she extended the grant for another eight months. And in 1971, I moved to London because Mr. Parisot helped me to get management there, which opened up the opportunity to play concerts in London and begin a career."

Kirshbaum had already caught the attention of the music world two years earlier as winner of a top prize in the first International Cassado Competition in Florence, and as the only Western cellist among the winners of the Tchaikovsky Competition the following year. He made his American debut at the Metropolitan Museum of Art in New York in 1976. I first heard him there on a subsequent visit when he performed the complete unaccompanied Bach Suites in two concerts.

I ask him how he manages to reconcile his teaching with his concert activities. "I have a wonderful arrangement with [RNCM]," he says. "I was concerned about devoting enough time and attention to my students, so I made it a condition from the beginning that my class would be kept small and that my students could come to me in London between my visits to Manchester. This way I can see them about every ten days, and when they have special projects, like competitions, I see them more often. We agreed to try it for a year and—well, I'm still there.

"I have been teaching as long as I can remember," he adds, "and I love it. When I was growing up in Tyler, I was the only cellist in town, so by the time I was about nine, my father had me begin to teach six- and seven-year-olds."

When Kirshbaum came to America in March 1998, it was on a mission that transcended national and cultural boundaries and seemed a synthesis of his artistic and pedagogical ideals: he was performing the Dvořák Cello Concerto with the Waseda Symphony Orchestra, the official student ensemble of Tokyo's Waseda University, on a tour that included concerts in Boston, Washington, and New York's Carnegie Hall. This was no ordinary student orchestra. Founded in 1913, its members are not aspiring musicians, since Waseda, though one of Japan's most prestigious universities, has no conservatory or music department; rather, these are students in other disciplines who pursue musical activities with extraordinary seriousness in their spare time.

Their competent and dignified conductor, Chikara Iwamura, also graduated from the university in an academic field but went to music school for eight years afterward and is now a professional musician. The group undertakes a world tour every third year; this was its fourth visit to America.

I felt that being a soloist with such an orchestra must require considerable adventurousness as well as a strong pedagogical inclination. Kirshbaum confirms this when I talk with him the morning after the Carnegie Hall concert. "One reason I like to play with young orchestras," he explains, "is that they are so enthusiastic, so receptive. They are willing to work with immense concentration because they are so eager to learn, improve, and do their best. The kids in this orchestra are incredibly well disciplined; they have great respect for authority, for institutions.

"As you know, the Dvořák Concerto is extremely difficult and I thought long and hard before I chose it, but I realized that something like a Haydn Concerto, which is so transparent and exposed in every orchestral part, would have been just as problematic in a different way. We only had two rehearsals, one on stage the day of the first concert and another the day before, and you can imagine how intensive that was! At first, many of the players were not clear about the shape, the architecture of the piece—which, for me, is terribly important—so I wondered how soon we would actually be able to start making music, or even talk about it. But it was fascinating for me to see how rigorously they applied themselves and how quickly their playing improved after the first reading. We went into great detail and enjoyed the process of working things out, and by the end of the first rehearsal, I felt we had come such a long way that we had actually developed an interpretation."

Indeed, at the concert the Dvořák came off remarkably well. Kirshbaum played beautifully, projecting great expressiveness; thanks to his warm, open personality, his rapport with the conductor and the young players was close. And like a true teacher, he offered leadership as well as support and encouragement. The orchestra's playing, here and in the rest of a very demanding program that included Stravinsky's famously difficult *Rite of Spring*, made up for what it lacked in professional polish with wholehearted goodwill and enthusiasm.

I ask Kirshbaum how he had managed to communicate with the orchestra across the language barrier. "Well," he says with a smile, "musicians can always find a way. There are so many musical terms that are really universal, and one can sing, and gesture, and demonstrate. Though I must say, I'm not accustomed to demonstrating a lot; I do very little of it in my lessons because I find that students can get intimidated or overwhelmed and just want to copy what they hear. Nor do I ever tell them to listen to records until they know a piece. But when words prove to be inadequate, it's a different situation."

To help me find out more about the Waseda Symphony, Kirshbaum has invited Iwamura, who speaks almost no English, and an orchestra violinist, who speaks it fairly well, to join us later in the interview. From them I learn that the players stay in the orchestra only as long as they attend the university, which means a substantial turnover every time a class graduates. While

many of them have studied music privately since they were very young, perhaps a third take up an instrument only when they enter the university. "I didn't know that," puts in Kirshbaum, amazed. "You mean they've only been playing for about three years?"

"Yes," replies Iwamura, "especially the winds, the second violinists, violists, and cellists."

The orchestra is trained by "advisors," professional musicians of the NHK Symphony Orchestra in Tokyo. The student orchestra has two four-hour evening rehearsals each week and gives four or five concerts a year throughout Japan, each with a different, ambitious program. "This is quite a commitment," Kirshbaum commented. Moreover, the members themselves are responsible for selling tickets. The concerts and programs, as well as the tours abroad, are arranged by an official of the university.

I ask Kirshbaum how his connection with the orchestra came about. "The American part of its world tour is arranged through Columbia Artists, who are my managers," he answers, "and it was they who suggested that I be its soloist in this country. I had no previous contact with the orchestra. Of course I knew its reputation, its history, and its organization, but we didn't meet until the day before the first concert. But you know, the same often happens when you are engaged to play in some small town with a professional orchestra. You don't necessarily know the quality of the players or the conductor beforehand. When you sit down for the first rehearsal, you either get a sense of rapport and it's wonderful, or you don't and it's just too bad. You take potluck, so to speak, in all these situations. But this time I particularly enjoyed it because the kids were so receptive and eager to learn."

No wonder: he had so much to offer and did it so generously. It was the same openheartedness that motivated Kirshbaum to create the Pierre Fournier Award and become artistic director of the International Cello Festival; as founder and guiding spirit, he describes both enterprises with enormous affection and enthusiasm. "I was a great admirer of Fournier and his artistry as a cellist, and, I am proud to say, I was also his friend. When he passed away in 1986, it was a great blow to all of us in Great Britain, where he was deeply loved and admired. So I wanted to do something to perpetuate his name, and an award seemed the best way to honor him. To finance it, I assembled 12 cellists who had been actively performing in England, and we gave a concert at the Wigmore Hall in London in October 1987, which raised something like £6,000. That became the seed money for the award."

I ask if the winner was chosen in a competition. "We don't call it a competition," he replies. "But the applicants do have to play an audition. There are two rounds. In the first, they play 15 or 20 minutes; four of them advance to the second round and play an entire 45-minute recital the next day. They choose their own program, because we feel that how they put it together already indicates the level of their artistry. And of course, they have to demonstrate the ability to sustain a 45-minute performance, so the second round is a much more severe test than the first.

"We give only one award—there are no first, second, or third prizes—but on occasion there has been no award, because we felt that no one was ready for it. Our criterion is very simple: would we want to go to Wigmore Hall to hear this young person play a whole recital that evening?"

Applicants must be British or studying in Great Britain, Kirshbaum explains, "because we wanted above all to encourage young British cellists." They have to submit tapes, and the top age limit is 28. The auditions take place in London and the jury is thoroughly international; in 1998 it included, in addition to Kirshbaum, Karin Georgian from Armenia, Steven Doane from the United States, and Eleanor Warren from England.

"The idea for the cello festival came out of the Fournier Award," Kirshbaum goes on. "After the 12 cellists' Wigmore Hall concert, one of my colleagues in Manchester who was also an admirer of Fournier's said to me, 'Why don't we do the same thing in Manchester?' And literally without thinking, I said, 'We've already done a concert; let's do a festival.' I didn't stop to consider what this would actually mean, or of the ramifications it would entail. At that moment, it seemed a good idea. So in the next six months, from October 1987 to April 1988, I organized the first International Cello Festival. Its basic purpose was to raise money for the Fournier Award, and if there was anything left over from that, it would go to the Jacqueline du Pré Memorial Fund.

"Well, we didn't raise a lot of money that first year, but we did raise a lot of expectations as to the potential of such a festival. People were very excited about it

RECORDINGS

BACH: Suites, BWV 1007–1012 (Virgin Classics ZDCB 45086).

BARBER: Concerto, Sonata. With Roger Vignoles, piano; Scottish Chamber Orchestra, Jukka-Pekka Saraste, cond. (Virgin Classics 59565).

BEETHOVEN: Piano Trio in B-Flat, Op. 97 ("Archduke"); Dvořák: Piano Trio in E Minor, Op. 90 ("Dumky"). With Peter Frankl, piano, cond. (BBC MM141).

BRAHMS: Double Concerto; Beethoven: Triple Concerto. With Pinchas Zukerman, violin; John Browning, piano; London Symphony Orchestra, Christoph Eisenbach, cond. (RCA Red Seal 68964).

BRAHMS: Piano Trios, Opp. 8, 87, 101; Piano Quintet, Op. 34. With Peter Frankl, André Previn, piano; György Pauk, violin; Yale String Quartet (EMI 73341).

continued...

and came to me left, right, and center, asking, 'When are you having the next one? What are you going to do next time?' And I said, 'Now wait a minute—in my mind, this was a one-time event to help pay for the Pierre Fournier Award.' But I got carried along by everyone's enthusiasm and began to think about all the things one could do with this festival, because I realized that we hadn't even begun to scratch the surface.

"However, there was one truly exciting thing we did that first year," he asserts. "At our Gala Concert, we had the six unaccompanied Bach Suites played by six different cellists. People had doubts about such a program, even musicians. Some of my colleagues at the college said, 'That's going to be a very long program; do you think anyone will come?' And I said, 'I'm sure it's going to be a fascinating, riveting experience.' Though I've heard a single cellist play all six Suites in one day, it could be argued that the homogeneity of style might induce a certain sameness and eventually make the music feel like just a torrent of notes. But with six different cellists, you have very different stylistic approaches—David Geringas, for example, played the D-Major Suite on a five-stringed cello, as indicated by Bach himself. In short, the concert passed in a flash."

In its second decade, the now-triennial festival is going stronger than ever. Presented in association with the BBC, it takes place in May in the same years as the Fournier Award auditions, whose winner is invited to give a recital and receive the award at the festival. It lasts five days and offers events of many kinds—recitals, chamber music, concertos with orchestra, lectures, films, and performances by young artists. All the artists, be they aspiring or established, practically donate their services, so the festival has raised tens of thousands of dollars for charity through the years. There is also a cello- and bow-making competition with its own award. Those interested in further information about the festival should contact Festival Administrator, The Grange, Clay Lane, Handforth, Cheshire SK9 3NR, England (phone/fax [44] 162-553-0140).

One of the festival's guiding principles is to bring together some of the finest cellists in the world to exchange ideas and inspire one another, as well as to offer gifted students the opportunity to interact with distinguished artist-teachers and to learn from them in master classes and workshops. I ask who is invited to apply. "We have a formula for that," Kirshbaum answers. "Students are nominated by each college and music school in England, including the so-called specialist schools, of which the Yehudi Menuhin School [in Stoke d'Abernon] is the best known. In addition, most of the festival's visiting artists teach somewhere, and we ask them to nominate two of their students. Last time, we had close to 50 students participating in 12 master classes and four performance-related workshops. There is no upward age limit, and since most of the players come from conservatories, the downward age limit is about 16. However, sometimes I will personally invite an exceptionally gifted younger person who comes to my attention through a private teacher."

Kirshbaum not only gets some of the most famous, sought-after cellists—such as Yo-Yo Ma, Janos Starker, Steven Isserlis, and Siegfried Palm—to participate in the festival, but several of them have come back year after year. Naturally, this is very gratifying to Kirshbaum. But, he adds, "There are so many wonderful cellists that I do try to invite different ones every time. This may be determined by the repertoire, by a given festival's thematic strands, or by a new work of particular interest that someone offers to perform. I take ideas from everybody; that's part of my management style. For example, I have a broad outline for the programs, an architectural shape I'd like to give them, and I present this to all the artists: 'This is the theme I have in mind. Could you suggest two or three works you'd be happy to play that would fit into it?' That's very different from telling them, 'This is the program—you play this, you play that,' which could lead to a lot of dissatisfaction."

Suppose everybody wants to play the same piece? "That could happen," he says, smiling. "I remember the year we did the Beethoven sonatas and variations, eight works in all. The choice was very

RECORDINGS

(continued)

ELGAR: Concerto. Royal Scottish National Orchestra, Sir Alexander Gibson, cond. (Chandos 8384 [1985] and 6607 [1979]).

HAYDN: Concerto, Hob. VIIb:2 in D. English Symphony Orchestra, Pinchas Zukerman, cond. (RCA Red Seal 62696).

TIPPETT: Concerto for Violin, Viola, Cello, and Orchestra. With György Pauk, violin; Nobuko Imai, viola; London Symphony Orchestra, Sir Colin Davis, cond. (Philips Classics 420 781).

WALTON: Belshazzar's Feast, Symphony No. 1. Scottish Festival Brass Bands, Sir Alexander Gibson, cond. (Chandos 2410).

WALTON: Concerto. Royal Scottish National Orchestra, Sir Alexander Gibson, cond. (Chandos 6547).

circumscribed. When I asked the players for their three choices, the A-Major Sonata, of course, was heavily favored."

However, Kirshbaum notes that the cello festival demonstrates a striking phenomenon: the proliferation of cellists and of cello music. He also declares, "Equally remarkable is the camaraderie, the spirit of collegiality and absence of competitiveness, among these people. After all, everyone who comes to the festival is very much an individual with a strong ego; that's what one needs to be a soloist. But the shared sense of treading this career path, which is very difficult, especially for a cellist, and the excitement of discovering new works—all this proves to be much stronger than any personal agenda.

"Let me tell you a story," he continues. "Four years ago, Starker was playing the cello version of the Bartók Viola Concerto. I was walking across the campus and met two very distinguished cellists of my own generation who had been listening to him rehearse it. We stopped and chatted and they spoke with an admiration bordering on amazement about what they had just heard him do. And I thought, how wonderful that top soloists like these should have the capacity to listen to another great cellist and react with so much appreciation!

"I feel that this spirit is one of the great things about the festival. In our gala concerts, we have seven or eight cellists sharing the program; it's a very long recital with a dinner break. And the artists who are not playing listen to their colleagues out in the hall, or else we put chairs for them right by the door where you come out of the dressing room. That curiosity on the one hand, and appreciation of one another's playing on the other, is a wonderful, wonderful thing."

WHAT HE PLAYS

Ralph Kirshbaum plays a Domenico Montagnana cello of 1729; he also has a G.B. Guadagnini cello made in Parma in 1765, and another by Vincenzo Panormo. His bows, in order of preference, are by Alfred Joseph Lamy, Charles Peccatte, François Nicolas Voirin, and John Dodd.

His strings, as of this interview, are Prim steel A and D and a Dominant synthetic G. He used to use an American Gold Label C, but, he says, "That company is now defunct, and I bought up the last of their supply. They are gut, wound, and have a particularly warm, radiant sound. Now I use Pirastro Permanente C strings, which I'm very happy with."

Laurence Lesser

9

LAURENCE LESSER BEGAN HIS CAREER as a highly successful young performer. Besides taking a top prize in the 1966 International Tchaikovsky Competition in Moscow, he graduated with honors in mathematics from Harvard, went on to study music in Germany on a Fulbright Scholarship, and then won first prize in the Cassado Competition in Siena, Italy. He made his New York debut recital in 1969. However, he has long been as passionate about pedagogy as performing, and his years as president of the New England Conservatory, which concluded just before this 1997 interview, put him on the map as a talented and committed teacher and arts administrator. He still teaches at NEC and continues to perform and record.

INDEPENDENT THINKER

Barbara Sealock

When cellist Laurence Lesser stepped down from a 13-year term as president of the New England Conservatory earlier this year, in January 1997, he completed a remarkable tenure star-studded with accomplishments. Now the educator—whose reputation as a performing artist is also well established—can put his full attention on his first love, teaching. In fact, Lesser finds coaching students an even greater reward than the considerable initiatives of his term as administrator of the country's second-ranked music school.

Those accomplishments are not to be glossed over, however. Lesser can justly claim credit for NEC's meteoric rise in the annual schools poll conducted by *U.S. News and World Report*. Although NEC has always had glittering assets, it took Lesser's vision and drive to make them shine and bring the venerable conservatory up to high expectations for the next millennium. Recent years have seen important additions to the NEC faculty, among them the world-renowned clarinetist Richard Stoltzman and classical guitarist Eliot Fisk. "And the quality of our students is just phenomenal," Lesser adds enthusiastically.

What pleases Lesser most about his administration's accomplishments was the highly-touted restoration of NEC's legendary acoustical jewel, Jordan Hall. "It cost us in excess of $8 million, and many years of planning," Lesser says. The goal was to modernize the hall, from making it handicapped-accessible to providing air conditioning. An architectural treasure on the National Historic Register said by some to be "an act of grace," Jordan Hall is "like a Stradivari," according to Lesser. "It sounds beautiful and seems to get better with age, provided it's lovingly cared for." He is not the only one who thinks so; such performers as cellist Yo-Yo Ma have also named it a favorite place to play, praising its intimacy and fine acoustics.

"We're on solid ground," Lesser says of NEC as a whole, reflecting on the successful $25-million capital campaign completed in 1995, the gala year marking the reopening of Jordan Hall in all its splendor. The years of fund-raising included the 1983 fulfillment of a $6-million Ford Foundation grant, a $1-million National Arts Stabilization Fund grant, and a $182,000 bestowal in 1985 from the National Endowment for the Humanities, with a $350,000 challenge grant that same year from the National Endowment for the Arts.

But for all of the hard-won capitalistic grandeur essential to NEC's survival and progress, the bottom line for Lesser is education. He continued to teach throughout his administrative term, and juggling the double agenda was never an issue. "I don't think I could have been president all these years had I stopped teaching," he explains. "It's a part of my soul. I love teaching, and I've been doing it uninterruptedly since 1964."

As an artist-teacher, Lesser has made an art of combining education with performance, and he finds that each discipline has something to offer the other. At present, he is working with 21 young cellists—more than a full-time load—and credits "terrific colleagues" such as soloist Colin Carr, Yee-Sun Kim (a cellist in NEC's resident Borromeo Quartet), and chamber musician David Wells for contributing to NEC's exhilarating learning environment.

Lesser's teaching career began at the age of 12, when he began coaching a schoolmate, a pianist who wanted to learn the cello. "The pupil is now a psychiatrist in Fresno who plays very avidly in a string quartet. I've had all different kinds of teaching experiences along the way," Lesser says. He taught students at Harvard while he was an undergraduate majoring in math, and he recalls that one of his most heady experiences was acting as Gregor Piatigorsky's assistant at the University of Southern California. "I was an assistant responsible for such extraordinarily gifted people as Jeffrey Solow, Stephen Kates, and Nathaniel Rosen. Although I was very close to them in age and didn't think I was their teacher, it gave me a wonderful opportunity to fool around with pedagogical ideas with people who could do just about anything.

"I think I know an awful lot by now about what to do and what not to do. The most fundamental thing I could say is that it's important that people learn to play the instrument physically in a way that as much as possible resembles their normal day-to-day behavior, so that when you pick up a cello you don't suddenly become some kind of a separate creature or monster. You really are trying to adapt what you do in a normal physical way to what you do on the instrument."

This issue of learning to play "naturally" is a central theme in Lesser's teaching philosophy. "One fundamental physical principle for

Lesser with Rostropovich.

my teaching deals with the fact that we are all prisoners, willing or not, of gravity," he explains. "The vertical direction of gravity to the surface is very important to our technique, and the chance to rest on the instrument, as appropriate, should be taken advantage of. So my way of talking about bow technique is to say the bow rests on the thumb and the fingers rest on the bow, rather than to say one holds the stick in such-and-such a way. And in the left hand, one tries to line up the fingers so that they are vertical, not perpendicular to the fingerboard, but vertical to the floor, so that one can best use that natural heaviness, in the direction in which it exists.

"In bow technique, while gravity is very useful to us, pushing straight down on a string makes no sound. A string really only vibrates sideways. The trick there is to learn how to apply weight to the sides of the string, so on the upbow, it's on the right side of the string; on the downbow, it's on the left side of the string, and not straight down on the string. It's often hard for people to understand that they can actually get a better result sometimes by doing less. My goal with this is that the technique should be liberating, not confining."

"I've studied a lot about how good players look when they play," Lesser continues, "and what's amazing to me is that the ones who are physically comfortable at the instrument, able to do things in a natural way, resemble each other enormously. One of the great confirmations of this came in 1967 when I went to play in the Casals Festival Orchestra in San Juan, Puerto Rico. My teacher, Piatigorsky, was invited, and there was a performance of the Schubert C-Major Quintet, in which both [Piatigorsky and Casals] played. At a rehearsal, I was absolutely startled to find that these two cellists resembled one another physically in how they approached the instrument. When you look at the great players—violin or viola or cello—you will find these same principles [are consistent] from one player to another."

Lesser says another of his most important teaching tenets is to help his students become independent. "What I'm most anxious to do," he explains, "is to give students this physical approach so they can be who they are as individuals. And in teaching pieces of music, I never initially give bowings and fingerings, because I want the students to develop their own ideas and try them out on me. Then if I think they're on the wrong track, that becomes the basis for discussion, which allows me to share with them ideas about how to approach problems. It's much broader in its usefulness than giving a particular answer to a particular problem.

"But what's most important to me is that they are who they are, not who I want them to be. They're individuals. I'm very proud of the fact that my students don't sound like one another. They're all very different people, and I pride myself on teaching every student differently. You have to figure out the personality of each one, and find a way of communicating with them that they'll understand—and that's natural to you, too.

"I guess my most important motto in teaching—and I announce it to all my students when they arrive—is that it's my goal to get rid of them," Lesser says with a smile. "Of course it sounds like a joke, but I'm serious. My ambition is to share what I know with a student, and get out of their way. It's like teaching someone to drive a car—you don't tell them where to go, and you don't go with them on the trip. I'm proud of my students, but I'm not possessive of them."

Lesser performing with colleagues.

In what ways did Piatigorsky influence his teaching style? "The vivid power of the way he played was overwhelming," Lesser responds. "I thought he was an intuitive natural player, and I learned a lot about what are good things to do just by watching him—but his approach to teaching was also very psychological, so that he would very often find the solution to a problem indirectly.

"The most famous example I can give you is this: There was a cellist who played in class one day whose tone was involuted, cramped, and uncommunicative. [Piatigorsky] simply made the person play the same thing over again, only he said, 'Now while you're playing it, I want you to look out the window.' Just with that one action, the change in the person's playing was enormous, because for the first time he was really listening to how he played. Also, he was not physically playing in a way that turned in on himself; he was opening out.

"That's one example. Piatigorsky was full of imagery in his teaching, and I am, too. I will often illustrate something by analogies to nonmusical things—everything from painting or literature to food, cooking, sports—it doesn't matter what. For instance, I'm sitting here in my office right now, and I'm looking at a large poster by Willem de Kooning. This painting is full of great swirls of color, and I might say to somebody, 'Look at that painting. Do you see that in order to create it, he must have moved his brush in such a fashion, and if you can push the bow just a little bit faster, or slow it down, or have more variety in it, you can create all kinds of different sounds?' I also love cooking and good food, and so my students know that I'm very apt to say that something doesn't have a meaty enough character, or it's not spicy enough, or it needs a touch of vinegar."

Lesser also thinks it is important to stress stylistic differences as well as tone production, intonation, articulation, and other usual teaching concerns. "So, for instance, if my students play a Bach cello suite, I want them to think about it as a piece by Bach," he says. "I may relate it to a Brandenburg Concerto or to the *St. Matthew Passion* or to some keyboard works, as opposed to just some étude for solo cello. In learning Beethoven, they obviously have to know about Beethoven as a pianist. I had a student play a Chopin sonata, and I said, 'Well, now, this is the scherzo movement. If you really want to know something about how this should go, don't look to another cello piece, go listen to a Rubinstein recording of mazurkas and waltzes, and you'll learn a lot about the characteristic of this composer and his rhythm and his kind of phrases.'

"The [students] are grateful," he adds, "because they're sometimes so busy in the practice room that they forget that they're playing an instrument, that the instrument is playing music, and the music is by different people. Sometimes just pointing that out frees them from a narrow perspective. I say, 'You see, it's Bach—it's not cello, it's Bach.'"

Lesser contends that these teaching goals serve all students well, whether or not they hope to become soloists. A good number of them, in fact, have a strong interest in joining orchestras. Lesser likes to supplement what he teaches those students by guiding them to other mentors.

RECORDINGS

AMERICAN MASTERS. Henri Lazarof: Concerto for Cello No. 1, *Continuum.* With the Oakland Symphony Orchestra, Gerhard Samuel, cond. (Composers Recordings 631).

A PORTRAIT OF FREDERICA VON STADE. Works by Mozart, Rossini, Chausson, et al. (Sony Classics 39315).

"Since I've never been a professional orchestra player," he explains, "I'm always happy when they have access to members of the Boston Symphony. There are tricks that I can't really help them with because I don't have that experience. However, there is a set of standard 'Top 40' orchestra excerpts, and I certainly know how to play them. I'm very aware of the orchestra literature and try as hard as I can to help them play in a basic, musical, technically sound fashion—and also in a flexible way, because when they play with different conductors, they have to be able to modify the way they play according to what the leader wants."

Lesser's students have done well. Katinka Kleijn, one of about 150 hopefuls who auditioned for the Chicago Symphony, landed a place as a section cellist in her first orchestral audition. "I was very proud of her," says Lesser. "I went over all the excerpts with her; and all the auditions also require a solo piece, which is definitely my territory. Candidates usually send a tape, and then they're either invited to come and play live—or not. Generally, in most orchestras, the first round is behind a screen, so there's no favoritism. And then, in her case, two or three finalists spent time with [music director] Daniel Barenboim to see whether he was pleased. And of course the players' committee had to recommend the person."

Carter Brey, now section leader with the New York Philharmonic, was one of Lesser's students when he taught at the Peabody Institute from 1970 to 1974. "When he came to me he'd only had formal cello lessons for three or four years—quite extraordinary," Lesser recalls. "He was about 17 at that time, and I admitted him on the basis of a tape I'd heard, which I thought showed extraordinary potential. He's a tremendously bright guy, a very charismatic player, and I think all those qualities are going to be of enormous benefit to him in the context of the New York Philharmonic."

Lesser also taught the Philharmonic's associate principal cellist, Alan Stepansky, when he was a student at Harvard. The orchestra's Elizabeth Dyson studied with Lesser and Bernard Greenhouse—making a total of three Philharmonic cellists from the same "stables," as Lesser puts it. He also coached Naumburg Competition–winner Andrés Díaz, who came to NEC at the age of 16 and stayed for six years. "At first he worked only with me," Lesser says, "and then when I became president, he worked with both me and Colin Carr. He's extraordinarily accomplished and gifted." Díaz went on to combine teaching at Boston University with a solo career. Another success story among Lesser's students is Sharon Robinson of the Kalichstein-Laredo-Robinson Trio, who studied with him at Peabody and now performs as both a chamber musician and a soloist.

Not surprisingly, Lesser is a strong believer in restoring music to the public schools and is committed to taking an active role in that effort. "The conservatory is involved in an extremely important program called the Boston Music Education Collaborative," he explains. "Our partners in that are the Boston Symphony, WGBH [Boston's public broadcasting station], and Boston's school system. Each organization is doing something different. We're not trying to do all the teaching, because there are fine teachers in the Boston schools, but we are trying to enrich what they're doing." In fact, members of the partnership have worked together to develop a music curriculum, and NEC faculty and students are supplementing the school's staff, which lost some music teachers during recent years of budget cutting.

In the midst of this hyperactive agenda, Lesser also expects to perform more himself. "It will probably take a little while to get it going, but I'm not a beginner," he says. "I'm sure I have something to bring to audiences, and I'm going to do my best to make sure that happens. Meanwhile I go to the Banff Centre for the Arts in the Canadian Rockies every June to coach chamber music and to play it. Chamber music is a very important part of my life as a performer and always has been. The Banff program resembles the Marlboro Music Festival in Vermont to a degree, at least in my participation, because I always try to involve myself with a group of younger players."

In this activity, Lesser says he is trying to pass along some of the good fortune he himself had as a young player. "I was very lucky because of early associations with [violinist Jascha] Heifetz and Piatigorsky. And while I don't put myself on the same pedestal they deserve to be on, an older, seasoned, experienced player has an awful lot to give playing in a group with younger, talented players. It's positive in both directions. The young player picks up much more, more quickly, by actually playing alongside someone older. A great deal of information can be grabbed intuitively, rather than through a lot of explanations and lessons. And I think the older player really enjoys the vitality of the younger ones, and the enormous sense of satisfaction that one is passing something along that is going to continue."

Lesser's activities as instructor and co-performer all contain various elements of teaching. And his most important message is that music is a form of communication. "Our young musicians always have to be aware of the fact that their role in life is to communicate," he says emphatically. "As long as they really understand that, and they're uninhibited and inventive in figuring out how they're going to communicate, I have unbounded optimism.

"Everything we've talked about—how you hold the bow, or how you think about the music—all of those are just ideas that serve this bigger theme, which is that we are here to communicate."

WHAT HE PLAYS

"I play a cello made in 1622 by the brothers Amati," says Lesser. "It's an instrument that was originally what they call a church bass, and it was slightly cut down in size, perhaps a hundred years ago. It has, to me, an extraordinarily beautiful sound.

"As for strings, I grew up playing on bare gut strings on A and D, and I have a fantasy that some day I'm going to go back to that. Steven Isserlis plays on bare gut strings, by the way. Heifetz used a bare gut A and D, I believe. But in any case, my A and D strings are currently metal. The C and G strings are silver-wound synthetic cores. I recently started using a Pirastro Permanent medium A next to a Jargar D medium, and Dominant silver G and C strings.

"The bow I play with was made by Dominique Peccatte about 150 years ago."

David Finckel

10

SOLOIST, RECITALIST, AND TEACHER David Finckel, who was born into a family of cellists, leads one of the most musically active lives imaginable—and he feels privileged to do so. As Mstislav Rostropovich's only American student, Finckel carries on the tradition of teaching while also filling many other roles, including member of a quartet, half of a sonata-duo, founder of a record label, father, administrator, and performer. In this fall 2000 interview, Finckel reflects on his accomplishments and begins to consider passing the torch to the next generation.

MARATHON MAN

Edith Eisler

I am very, very fortunate," says cellist David Finckel. "Very few people are afforded so many opportunities to play on such a high level. When people become successful and play a lot, they sometimes forget that the opportunity to play is the most precious gift any musician can have. Take that away and it's like taking the air from someone who needs to breathe. As a cellist and a musician, I can't imagine a better life." No wonder: it is filled with more musical activities than most people would try to fit into one lifetime. Finckel is the cellist of the Emerson String Quartet (whose other members are Eugene Drucker and Philip Setzer, violinists, and Laurence Dutton, violist), which gives more than 100 concerts a year worldwide and is constantly adding to its already substantial discography. Finckel also plays solo recitals and concertos with orchestras, and he and his wife, pianist Wu Han, are partners in a sonata duo as well as in a record company, ArtistLed, which they established together. The two accepted the artistic directorship of SummerFest La Jolla in California in 1998, then relinquished it after the 2000 season because of disagreements with the parent organization, the La Jolla Chamber Music Society. The two players, who celebrated their 15th anniversary last September, have a six-year-old daughter, Lily, who already studies the piano.

I have spoken with David Finckel several times over the years, and most recently we discussed the interaction and balance between the different components of his extraordinarily multifaceted career.

Tell me something about your background. I know you studied with Rostropovich—

—yes, and also with Bernard Greenhouse—

—but how and when did you get started?

Well, first of all, there is a lot of music in my family.

And a lot of cellists, but I've never been able to figure out how they're related.

I can tell you that! The two who are active, Michael and Chris, are my cousins. Their father, George, was a cellist and a member of many distinguished groups; he taught at Bennington College for many years. I also have grandfathers and uncles who were cellists: my great-uncle Alden was principal cellist of the National Symphony under Hans Kindler. And in my family cellists traditionally married pianists, long before I did.

I grew up in New Jersey; my father, Edwin, was a composer and taught piano and wind instruments in the school I attended, a wonderful, very progressive private school based on education through the arts. I was at school with him all week, soaking up music and art, and on weekends he taught privately at home; I would hear his students' lessons and socialize with them afterward. I learned basic theory and could play the piano quite well before I began to study the cello at about 10 or 11, which is relatively late.

I was very fortunate with my teachers. The first one, Mary Gili, was a wonderful teacher and a real taskmaster. She put me through the [David] Popper Etudes and the [Friedrich] Dotzauer books; I credit her with a lot of my basic technique. Then I studied with Elsa Hilger, a member of the Philadelphia Orchestra, who was also wonderful. I was rather shy as a child and a young musician; though I loved to play in front of people, I didn't like taking risks, but Elsa Hilger was extremely enthusiastic and pushed me to take some competitions.

I met Rostropovich at Elsa Hilger's home. He was playing with the Philadelphia Orchestra; she took me in for the week and I went to all his rehearsals and concerts. She invited him to dinner and afterward I played the Schumann Concerto for him. Needless to say, that was a turning point for me. Thereafter, he was always very good to me and would hear me play whenever I asked him to. I studied with him on and off for maybe nine years, in Europe, in America. I just followed him around. Sometimes we met in odd places and at odd hours of the day, but he never asked for anything in return. I practiced so hard for those lessons! It was in preparing for them, as much as in the lessons themselves, that I really learned to play the cello. He once told me that when, in practicing, you find something you cannot do, that is your luckiest moment. The most essential thing to look for in a difficult passage is what's holding you back, even if it's only one or two notes;

then you know what to improve, to fix. Rostropovich suggested that I go to the Tchaikovsky Competition in Moscow; I practiced very hard for it for about six months, and then became so frightened that I backed out.

I was also fearful of taking auditions, but I was persuaded to try out for the Colonial Symphony Orchestra in Madison, New Jersey, where I soon became principal cellist, succeeding my old teacher Mary Gili. This happened to be the year when [violinist] Oscar Shumsky became the orchestra's music director and brought with him many of his Juilliard students. Some were fantastic players, and one of them was Philip Setzer, so this was where I had my first contact with members of the Emerson Quartet.

RECORDINGS

BEETHOVEN: Complete Works for Piano and Cello. With Wu Han, piano (ArtistLed 19801-2).

EDWIN FINCKEL: Music for Cello. With Wu Han, piano (ArtistLed DF-93847).

GRIEG: Sonata in A Minor; Schumann: Adagio and Allegro; Chopin: Sonata in G Minor. With Wu Han, piano (ArtistLed 19701-2).

STRAUSS: Sonata in F Major, Op. 6; Franck: Sonata in A Major; Finckel: Variations. With Wu Han, piano (ArtistLed 19602-2).

TCHAIKOVSKY: Trio in A minor, Op. 50; Kodály: Duo for Violin and Cello, Op. 7. With Da-Hong Seetoo, violin; Wu Han, piano (ArtistLed 19601-2).

When did you join the quartet?

In the 1979–80 season; I must have been 27 or 28.

When you already had a considerable solo career. Did you put it on hold?

Let's say I was distracted by the quartet. During our first two seasons, we learned and performed more than 70 pieces, including all the Beethoven and Bartók quartets, several Mozarts, countless Haydns. The first year I was in the quartet, we played 60 or 70 concerts; it took me several years just to become used to that.

How soon did you go back to playing solo?

I had kept it going, of course, though the quartet became a major part of my life. But it was meeting Wu Han that was a pivotal experience for me. She played with the quartet as winner of a student competition at the Hartt School of Music, where we were teaching; her playing spoke to me immediately and very soon I asked her if she would play a recital with me. The first sonata I picked was the Chopin; it's extremely romantic and needs to be played with a lot of technique, but also with a kind of instinctive, natural feeling. It's the kind of piece that's likely to sound self-conscious if you talk about it and analyze it too much. I'd played it with many pianists and had always searched for somebody with whom I could play the repertoire without having to talk too much in rehearsal. Wu Han and I couldn't communicate too well anyway, because she didn't speak much English at the time. The performance was very successful and from then on we began a steady crescendo of duo activity. In recent seasons, the duo has played almost half as many concerts as the quartet. I can never play too many solo and duo concerts—I absolutely love doing it. And fortunately, many of these dates are with Wu Han, so the more concerts I play, the more my family is actually together; we've even taken Lily along on tour.

She gets to see the world early in life!

She loves it, but she does get confused sometimes. [*Laughs.*] One of the first things I did with Wu Han was unusual for me: in 1985 I played in a competition, the New England Conservatory Piatigorsky Prize. It was awarded not only for solo playing, but also for chamber music and teaching. There were four contestants, and we all played a duo recital. I played some chamber music with the faculty at NEC and also taught a master class in front of the judges. That was very interesting and challenging, because on the jury were Laurence Lesser, Bernard Greenhouse (with whom I had studied) and Raya Garbusova (whom I greatly admired). I was fortunate enough to win the competition, much against my expectations.

Tell me a bit more about Wu Han. Where did she study and what did she do before she met you?

She grew up in Taipei and was a very precocious young musician. Though the quality of music teaching in Asia has risen, the students often receive a great deal of technical training but have to catch up on their musical education when they come to the West. The basic practice is to get elementary training at home and then go to the United States or Europe for further study. I think this has a lot to do with careers: if you want a good teaching job in Taiwan, you'll get twice the salary if you have a degree from an American school.

When did Wu Han come to America?

I believe in 1981; she was 22. She came to study with Raymond Hanson at the Hartt School. Then, through the quartet, she met many musicians and became known through her participation in summer festivals: she played for [pianist] Leon Fleisher in Aspen, for [violinist] Felix Galimir at Marlboro, and also for [pianist] Lilian Kallir. In some ways, she was not a typical Asian student. She didn't fit into a mold, and she is very Western and freethinking in her spirit. She is a big risk taker, unlike me; she thrives on taking chances. That's been very good for me, and for the duo.

I think I can tell that from the way you two play together.

Yes, the experience ignited the pent-up soloist and duo cellist in me, and then one thing led to another, musically and also personally—but not until later. The origins of our relationship are musical.

And she is also your partner in your record company.

It's not a record company like any other that I know of. The key difference is that we don't advertise; we have no marketing department. The records are not sold through stores but through a toll-free number [(800)582-1699], through our Web site [www.artistled.com], and at our concerts. The label is called ArtistLed because the artists really control everything. The records are produced by Wu Han and me in cooperation with our engineer, Da-Hong Seetoo, who is a violinist and a graduate of the Juilliard School and the Curtis Institute.

We have our own way of recording: our engineer sets the sound and leaves, and we record alone. We're our own producers and editors, and we choose every note that goes on the recordings ourselves. We don't tell anyone what records we're going to make, so we're under no pressure to release—if it doesn't work, or if we don't like what comes out, we just throw it away. We can record what we want when we feel the time is right for us. The most important thing to us is to record the music we love, to make something that is beautiful; I can't imagine recording the cello literature in any other way.

We've had the label for about three years. Obviously, for us, making records is not about making money; it's about preserving our interpretations. When you get to a certain age you begin to think, "Well, maybe I won't play this piece so well in two years," or, "I feel so good about this piece now that I'd love to capture a performance of it." That's what happened with our Beethoven sonatas—we felt it was the right moment to make the records, and it turned out to be wonderful to have them. Last July, we performed the cycle five times and it was great to have the records there at the concerts where people could buy them; it's the most natural place to sell a recording.

Are you one of the first to found such a label?

I may have been one of the first to do it in a formal way, but on some level it's been going on for a long time, especially among jazz and rock 'n' roll players; they were far ahead of the classical musicians in terms of artistic freedom and flexibility in the recording industry. And look at [pianist] Glenn Gould: he simply retreated from the concert scene because he found that in the recording studio he could control a whole world—and did he ever control it! He made a phenomenal success of it, professionally if not personally. What's great for me is that I have two recording lives, my own and the one with the quartet, which still has an exclusive contract with Deutsche Grammophon. I guess having four Grammys is not a bad track record; we've seen executives come and go, but we're still there!

Didn't you record the Schubert Quintet with Rostropovich some years ago?

Yes! That was one of the highlights of my life. We recorded it in a beautiful old wooden church with the most incredible acoustics, in a little town in Germany named Speyer, near Mannheim. It was in the wintertime. The townspeople knew of our project and closed off the main street to accommodate us. We had made a take of the slow movement in the afternoon, and when we listened to it, Rostropovich said, "That doesn't sound right; one can't record this music in the daytime. Let's all go back to the hotel, sleep a couple of hours, and then come back in the evening." Of course, this being Rostropovich, we did what he said. When we got back that evening, it was completely quiet; the snow had begun to fall very heavily and was covering everything. We went into the

church with our producer, and in this magical setting, surrounded by this white blanket of snow, we recorded the slow movement. I'll never forget that feeling—the snow, the church, the music, and having my teacher sitting next to me and drawing on his incredible energy and inspiration.

How do you coordinate the quartet's concerts and your own? Your life must be a constant juggling act.

Well, you plan your seasons, put the dates in, and then figure out how to get from one place to another. You take the opportunities that are too good to turn down. It happens that I'll come to my partners and say, "I have an offer to go on tour for a week two years from now," and they'll look at me and say, "Oh, David, how are we going to rehearse?" Well, you can be sure that when the time comes, they'll be happy to have a week off while I go and work. It gives the quartet a very needed break; we all have families and responsibilities besides our instruments. And I think it's good for all of us to have the freedom to go off and do other things. Some quartets don't like that, but ours isn't one of them. Phil and Gene also play solo and concerto dates; Phil played the Shostakovich Concerto last summer with the Aspen Orchestra, and Gene came to my festival.

Of course it can be exhausting. I've found myself flying back and forth between, say, Texas and Boston to play a quartet date between other engagements. That kind of thing is really crazy, and I try to avoid it if I can. But there's such joy in playing and making music. It's not just a profession; it's a great life that has very positive human rewards. My passport to the musical world is the cello. It is my first and greatest musical love, the axis around which I balance everything: the duo, the quartet, the family. And somehow each feeds on the others.

Within the last five years, I've developed so much more confidence in myself that I'm actually quite comfortable in front of the public. Playing the great quartet literature has been a tremendous musical education. As violinist Isaac Stern said, you can learn everything you need to know about music through chamber music: how it's put together, what's important, how to solve problems, how to make a piece work. I also feel I have so much more practical musical knowledge than in the early days, just from the number of solo concerts I've played, including many repeat performances of the same pieces. Now when I go out on stage as a soloist, I'm in a position to take chances in all kinds of situations, and really enjoy myself to a much greater degree than ever before in my life, and a lot of the credit for that goes to Wu Han.

Where did you acquire the organizational skills needed to run a summer festival?

That goes back to my early teens. When I was 10 or 11 years old, my parents bought a piece of land in Vermont to establish a music camp. We built it really from the ground up; my father and I put up many of the buildings ourselves. My mother did all the cooking for 16 years— three meals a day for as many as 60 to 75 people—with hardly any help. It was a very family-run operation; I helped with everything, working behind the scenes, and at a very early age I became involved with organizing theory classes, chamber-music groups, scheduling. I gravitated toward the administrative end, because my father was more concerned with the maintenance of the place and other practicalities. My parents used me as a confidante, so I knew about all of the musical as well as the personal and practical problems and issues of dealing with a large group of people.

What happened to that camp?

It still exists after 30-some years, under its third set of owners. It's a very popular chamber music camp called Point CounterPoint.

So, four years ago, when Wu Han and I accepted the directorship of SummerFest La Jolla, I found that I was slipping very naturally back into the old role I'd had in my parents' camp, planning programs, organizing activities, putting musicians together, and so on. Wu Han and I had participated in many festivals, including SummerFest in 1992, '94, and '96, so we knew the place and the community; we knew how the festival ran, and we had lots of ideas about what we wanted to keep and what to change.

I've heard very good things about it.

Oh yes! We were given very wide creative latitude and asked to put La Jolla on the map as a cultural destination, and indeed many people were beginning to find visiting it worth the journey. I think we tried to create a sort of musical utopia where, whether you came for the whole three weeks of the festival or for only a short time, every day would be a very rich experience. We brought in not only the very finest players for the concerts, but also three young ensembles whom they coached in sessions that were free to the public. There were discussions on various issues pertaining to the world of the arts, like education, funding, recording, [the music] industry. We tried very hard to bring in outside journalists who would report home on the festival; they came from Germany, England, Mexico, Canada. We enjoyed incredible enthusiasm from the press, support from the public, generosity from the community, and the help of a very dedicated, resourceful committee of volunteers. On the whole, running the festival was an amazing experience for us; the quality of the artists, the speakers, the music making, was incredible, and we felt privileged to be part of it. But I'm not in a hurry to find something to take its place. I think it's healthy to have a period of time for reflection and planning.

Does being the son of a teacher, and having been around all those students at your parents' camp for so many summers, give you the urge to be a teacher yourself?

Well, it did make me feel I was on the teachers' side of the fence rather than the students', even when I was still quite young and a student myself. I always seemed to see things from the teacher's perspective. I'm not teaching regularly at present, but I conduct master classes and I've taken part in Isaac Stern's chamber-music workshops in both New York and Jerusalem. However, at some time I'll want to go into real teaching. This came up in discussion with the quartet one day last summer after Oscar Shumsky passed away. He had given a tremendous amount of wisdom to our two violinists, and we realized we're all now

at an age when our teachers are starting to disappear, or to stop teaching, as Shumsky did (he was very reclusive). You not only want to carry on your teacher's work; if you've built your own musical principles on what you've learned and you have something that you feel is good and right and meaningful, you want to pass it on, the way they pass the Olympic torch. When we think of our mentors, they're all quite elderly, and many are gone—Galimir, [pianist Rudolf] Serkin, [violinist Alexander] Schneider—and yet we quote them in rehearsal

WHAT HE PLAYS

David Finckel uses a Sartory bow and also a modern bow by the Canadian maker Bernard Walke. His strings are Thomastik, a combination of Spirocores and Bel Cantos.

He has several cellos; the most famous is a Giovanni Battista Guadagnini made in Milan in 1754. But the one he uses most often was made by Samuel Zygmuntowicz in Brooklyn in 1993. There is quite a story attached to it.

"Some years ago, Gene Drucker came into a quartet rehearsal and started playing on the other side of the room," recalls Finckel. "We recognized that it wasn't his violin, but it sounded fantastic and looked beautiful. We all thought it was a Golden Period Strad, but when we finally asked, he said, 'It's a Samuel Zygmuntowicz, finished two weeks ago in Brooklyn.' He was trying it out and eventually bought it."

"Well, I just fell in love with its sound—it spoke to me somehow—so I decided to see if this man would make a cello for me. I talked to him, and he said that the cello he would be most anxious to copy was the famous 'Duport' Antonio Stradivari, which belongs to Mstislav Rostropovich. I knew that Rostropovich doesn't usually allow people to copy his instrument, but I showed him Gene's violin and he was so impressed that he agreed.

"It took Sam two years to find the right wood to match the Strad perfectly, and it took him five years to finish the cello. It was his first cello and I didn't know what to expect, but it turned out to be fantastic from the first day I played it. When I took it into the quartet, the others asked me, 'What Strad is that?' and finally I told them. That's what I usually do; I don't tell people what the cello is until they've heard it. At our concerts, half the time the program will say I'm playing the Guadagnini, and half the time the as freely as if they were still here. But the students of the new generation barely know who these people were; they missed what we got from them. So I feel the torch is coming into our hands, and it's our responsibility to hand it on. And I think I have something very special to give: I've been able to bring my quartet experience into the solo literature, and what's more, I have what I got from Rostropovich, and that's very unusual for an American cellist. So I feel there's another huge door that's opening a crack, and there's a very bright light shining through it.

Zygmuntowicz, though of course it's always Sam's cello. People come backstage and ask to see the Guadagnini, and I tell them it's not a Guadagnini, so they look inside and see a Strad label (which I had asked Sam to put in), and they drool over it, and then I tell them what it really is. I enjoy that, because I think people should use their ears, not their opinions about what's supposed to sound good.

"The cello has also contributed to giving me more self-confidence. It speaks out in a big, uncomplicated voice, strong and affirmative, and forces me to be that way myself. For a rough, aggressive player, it's better to have a sweet-sounding instrument, but I find that with this cello, it is possible to play a recital with a nine-foot piano that's open for pieces like the Rachmaninov or the Chopin Sonata. And Sam is becoming really popular: Phil is now using a Zygmuntowicz as well, a copy of Shumsky's Strad, a wonderful instrument. It blends better with Gene's Strad than the Lupot he used to play. This summer at the festival, there were five Zygmuntowicz instruments among the musicians.

"I really believe in today's young instrument makers," Finckel concludes. "I think they are going to save us, as old instruments are being increasingly priced out of the range of performers. Not only are they making better and better instruments, but they are a wonderful group of dedicated, hard-working people whose lives are centered on timeless values: patience, craftsmanship, and beauty. To see the expressions on their faces when I take their instruments and play them and bring them to life is one of the greatest rewards I can have as a cellist."

Yo-Yo Ma

11

CELLIST YO-YO MA IS ONE OF THE BEST LOVED performers of his or any other time. Chinese by parentage, French by birth, American by training and adoption, he is a true citizen of the world, to whom the exploration of every national, cultural, and artistic tradition comes naturally, especially since he is endowed with not only a superb musical gift, but also an extraordinarily inquiring, adventurous mind. His father started him on the cello when he was four; after coming to New York, he studied with Leonard Rose at the Juilliard School, and he also took a liberal-arts degree at Harvard University. This chapter is the result of two conversations with Ma; the first took place in Tanglewood in 1991 and the second via telephone in February 2001.

CONTINUITY IN DIVERSITY

Edith Eisler

Whehen I tell people that I interviewed Yo-Yo Ma, they all ask the same question: "Is he really as nice as he seems?" The answer is, "No, much nicer." His sunny charm and embracing warmth are absolutely genuine, not part of a public persona, and flow from some deep, inner source of human caring. Knowing that I do not drive, he came to my hotel in Tanglewood, and he telephoned me from his home in Boston. Open to both people and ideas, unspoiled by his superstar status, he is completely natural, unassuming, and eager to learn; indeed, the word *learn* runs through his conversation like a Leitmotif. In a notoriously competitive, slippery profession, not a disparaging word is ever heard either from him or about him. He is one of those rare people who can make even a hardened cynic believe that artistic and personal integrity go together.

Ma's multifaceted performing career includes playing concertos, recitals, and chamber music of all kinds; he just celebrated the silver anniversary of his sonata partnership with pianist Emanuel Ax by giving a wonderful Avery Fisher Hall recital. His repertoire ranges from Baroque to contemporary and is not confined to the standard literature: he has made forays into jazz with Stéphane Grappelli and Bobby McFerrin, Appalachian folk fiddling with Mark O'Connor and Edgar Meyer, Argentinean tangos by Piazzolla, and electronic music with computers by Tod Machover. His current, perhaps most ambitious, undertaking is the Silk Road Project, which explores "cross-cultural influences among and between the lands comprising the legendary Silk Road and the West."

Lesser men and musicians might be suspected of engaging in these adventures to generate publicity, but Ma gets so deeply involved with his projects and absorbs them into his life and his art so successfully that his sincerity is never in doubt. As he talks about them, a connecting thread emerges despite their diversity, which he describes as "a linear continuum in the pursuit of learning something." Here are some of the thoughts and reflections he shared with me on the challenges and joys of making and exploring music.

With your big solo career, how did you get into playing so much chamber music?

Because I loved it. There was always music in my family, but I grew up pretty lonely. The first time I was among kids who loved music was at Meadowmount, Galamian's summer camp. I was 15 and when they wanted to play late Beethoven in the middle of the night I went nuts, it was so exciting.

The next year I went to Marlboro for the first of four summers, and I think my love for chamber music really developed in those two places. I believe that whatever you play, even concertos, is basically chamber music. You always have to find out what your function is, whether you're playing an inner, upper, or lower voice. It's how you balance things out that's exciting to me.

Since you collaborate so closely with Mr. Ax—I've heard you many times and it's always wonderful—how does it feel to play with other partners?

It keeps your mind open, your ears fresh. You realize they've been searching for the same things and can meet you at midpoint; you try to create something special with each of them by using every available accommodation of strengths and abilities. I must say, however, that working with Manny (Ax) has meant an incredible friendship and an incredible joy, because after all this time we know so many layers of each other that there's a shorthand of communication—we can trust each other to say anything and know it's understood. We can rehearse just before a concert and decide what aspect of the music to go for; there's always freedom to improvise, and that encourages us to be creative. Playing together makes us so happy that, no matter how busy we are, we save time for it every year. Lately we've also played piano quartets with Isaac Stern and Jaime Laredo.

Haven't you played chamber music with Gidon Kremer as well?

Yes; he's an unbelievably interesting person to work with, one of the most creative, experimental violinists around, always daring himself to do more, digging deeper, challenging other people, getting them mad and himself upset—it's great! That's one of our goals as musicians, to explore, and he certainly does that.

SELECTED RECORDINGS

APPALACHIA WALTZ. With Edgar Meyer, bass; Mark O'Connor, violin (Sony Classical 68460).

BACH: Suites for Unaccompanied Cello (Sony Classical 37867).

BEETHOVEN: Concerto for Piano, Violin and Cello in C Major, Op. 56. With Daniel Barenboim, piano; Itzhak Perlman, violin; Berlin Philharmonic Orchestra, Itzhak Perlman, cond. (EMD/EMI Classics 55516).

BRAHMS: Concerto for Violin and Cello in A minor, Op. 102. With Itzhak Perlman, violin; Chicago Symphony Orchestra, Daniel Barenboim, cond. (Wea/Atlantic/Teldec 15870).

continued...

And so do you! I remember your concert with Grappelli.

I wanted to experiment with improvisation and I was scared. People used to improvise all the time, and I think the music schools should train us in it, because all playing should have an improvised quality. Playing with Bobby McFerrin was even scarier: we invented a four-minute piece, but he helped and encouraged me and it was great! When you're making things up, you're having fun; you're being playful.

Was that also what attracted you to the Appalachian adventure with Mark O'Connor and Edgar Meyer? Was most of that music written down or improvised?

Mark is a natural improviser, so most of the improvisation came from him. As for me, I'm comfortable trying it in a private environment, but hardly feel equipped to do in public. The reason I wanted to hook up with them was that I thought they were both phenomenal. I heard Mark play at Grappelli's 80th birthday concert at Carnegie Hall; I went backstage and said, "Can you teach me?" Eventually we got together and the first thing we decided was that we needed a lot of time.

So we'd meet somewhere about every month and, to me, every meeting was very exciting; the music sounded really wonderful and I thought I was doing pretty well. But not well enough for Mark and Edgar. Mark hadn't taught me very much, but I could see he wasn't happy with what was coming out of my cello. Edgar is more verbal, and he could explain what specifically I was doing wrong. It took me a long time to satisfy them.

What did you have to do?

I had to learn a whole different style of playing, in terms of intonation, and even more in terms of rhythm. The idea of rubato is deeply ingrained in much classical music; we think that time, with harmony as a pillar, can be bent slightly when playing a melody, a motive, or an interval. I realized that Mark and Edgar have a different set of priorities. What's of highest value to them is absolute precision, a groove-like rhythm that's very hard for a classical musician to acquire; it demanded a real cultural switch.

Then, for Edgar, over-vibrating is a terrible thing, so I found myself remembering the time when I was listening to Casals and wondering how he achieved such incredible expressivity with so little vibrato. I'm trained to play in 2,700-seat halls, to project, and vibrato of course helps the sound projection. This was closer to Baroque, and I also changed my bow grip toward a much more Baroque feel.

With which you were familiar from playing Baroque cello. How did you transform your Strad into a Baroque instrument, apart from taking out the endpin and putting on gut strings?

I used a different bridge and tailpiece. I could have changed the bass bar and used a shorter neck, but I didn't want to do that: it was too radical. The basic idea was to remove pounds and pounds of pressure from the cello by using different materials to produce sound. I also played with a Baroque bow; it took a good deal of adjustment and meant getting into a different sound world.

In the history of classical music, the rate of change in Europe since 1500 was astronomical, but before that it was much slower. When you strip away some of the innovations of the last 500 years and get into a pre-1600 playing mode, you can relate to other styles and instruments. I learned about

that from playing with Mark and Edgar. I also discovered that there are common elements between folk fiddling and Bach. Think of the drone and the way Bach uses pedal notes. In the second Gavotte of the Sixth Suite, you hear bagpipes, because at that time, people in the cities were looking for an idealized rural environment, and Bach wanted to evoke

SELECTED RECORDINGS

(continued)

CHOPIN: Cello Sonata; Trio. With Emanuel Ax, piano; Pamela Frank, violin (Sony Classical 53112).

CORIGLIANO: Phantasmagoria. With Emanuel Ax, James Tocco pianos (Sony Classical 60747).

DVORAK: Concerto for Cello in B minor, Op. 104/B 191; Victor Herbert: Concerto for Cello No. 2 in E minor, Op. 30. New York Philharmonic Orchestra, Kurt Masur, cond. (Sony Classical 67173).

GERSHWIN: Prelude for Piano No. 3 in E-Flat minor. With Jeffrey Kahane, piano (Sony Classical 64060).

HAYDN: Cello Concerto No. 1. English Chamber Orchestra, José-Luis Garcia, cond. (MK 44924).

MOZART: Quartet for Piano and Strings No. 2 in E-Flat Major, K 493; Quartet for Piano and Strings No. 1 in G minor, K. 478. With Emanuel Ax, piano; Jaime Laredo, viola; Isaac Stern, violin (Sony Classical 66841).

continued...

a country atmosphere. Drones are all over classical music, all over Celtic music, in fact all folk music.

Have you returned the Strad to its normal state?

No, it's still a Baroque instrument. Working with Ton Koopman's Amsterdam Baroque Orchestra was a great opportunity for me. The repertoire is so rich and beautiful, I want to continue to play it.

But for the Bach Suites you didn't use a Baroque instrument.

No, I just hold the bow slightly differently and sometimes tune low.

I've heard you play them many times and always loved it; I've also seen the film series Inspired by Bach. Would you tell me how that came about?

Essentially, the idea was to ask, What is a piece of music? I think its materiality is much more than just the notes. It's a code that opens a door to a world everybody interprets differently, because our aesthetic and sensory values are different and each generation has to discover its own.

So we said, Suppose we regard a piece of music as almost genetic material, like DNA, to the mind of a person who is both very receptive and imaginative. How would that person think of it, not in terms of the cello, but of their own medium? So for Julie Messervy, who is a garden designer and a family friend, the First Suite became a garden, a living thing, which, like a piece of music, only exists if it's nurtured. And it now exists in Toronto, as a concert hall without walls, a place where people partake in its living form, and it's absolutely gorgeous.

The Second Suite film was inspired by the fact that Bach actually tried to do the impossible: to create polyphonic music on a single-line instrument. The idea came from François Girard, who had directed *The Red Violin* and films about Glenn Gould. He is a very creative person and he wanted to do something on architecture. He chose Piranesi, because he, too, tried the impossible: to design structures that could in fact not be built. But François made them exist in virtual form in the film. And in the Sixth Suite, the ice dancers Torvill and Dean, who are great favorites in my household, also did on film what is physically impossible in reality: to skate [perfectly] for 27 minutes.

For the Third Suite, Mark Morris created a dance with incredibly masterful, inventive choreography. When we perform it, I feel the dancers are living notes; as I watch them, I am literally reading the text, and we sense a very profound interactivity. Mark took the code of, say, irregular patterns, and then superimposed his own irregular code on Bach's patterns; this breathed a different life into the piece without taking anything away from it. The work continues to live in the company's repertoire, and that makes me very happy.

The Fourth Suite film explores the question, How does a piece of music exist in a society? How does it live within a person who is ill, or an amateur musician, or someone who becomes absolutely obsessed with it? The Fifth Suite film asks, What does this music have in common with the world of Kabuki? Tamasaburo, a dancer I've admired for a long time, took almost a year to get inside the piece; finally, it was the idea of a candle, of lighting something, and also of the flames being gradually extinguished, that was the unifying factor for him, visually and choreographically. The result was a feeling of resignation, of giving up, but of still nurturing that fire, that life in the piece.

One of the most interesting aspects of the film project was collaborating with so many people—directors, filmmakers, writers—over a five-year period. I learned that there are two components to this. One is that you have to take time, lots of time, to let an idea grow from within. The second is that when you sign on to something, there will be issues of trust, deep trust, the way the members of a string quartet have to trust one another. Things can fall apart, or threaten to, for many reasons, and then there's got to be a leap of faith. Ultimately, when you're at the edge, you have to go forward or backward; if you go forward, you have to jump together.

For me, those two lessons and working together with all those idealistic, dedicated people constituted a second college degree. It took me way beyond what I knew, into places of which I was totally scared, but as I became less frightened, I welcomed new ways of thinking and approaching something. It made me an infinitely richer person, and I think a better musician. No matter what people said about the project—and it raised a lot of eyebrows—I'll never regret having done it.

I actually got the courage for the Bach project from two earlier experiences. One was a symposium called "What Is the Meaning of Schweitzer's Life in the 1990s?"

SELECTED RECORDINGS

(continued)

RACHMANINOV: Sonata for Cello and Piano in G minor, Op. 19; Sonata for Cello and Piano in C Major, Op. 119. With Emanuel Ax, piano (Sony Classical 46486).

SAINT-SAENS: Concerto for Cello No. 1 in A minor, Op. 33. ORTF National Orchestra, Lorin Maazel, cond. (Sony Classical 46506).

SCHUBERT: Quintet for Strings in C Major, Op. 163/D 956. With the Cleveland String Quartet (Sony Classical 39134).

SHOSTAKOVICH: Trio for Piano and Strings No. 2 in E minor, Op. 67; Sonata for Cello and Piano in D minor, Op. 40. With Emanuel Ax, piano; Isaac Stern, violin (Sony Classical 44664).

arranged by Mark Wolf, a federal judge in Boston and the head of the Albert Schweitzer Foundation. He invited musicians, doctors, social workers, theologians—members of the professions in which Schweitzer was active—to meet for a weekend and talk about him. He asked me to talk about Bach, so I had to reread many of Schweitzer's books. That weekend made me realize that, just like Bach, these people were all trying to do something impossible, because the work of a doctor, a social worker, a theologian, is never finished.

The other was a lecture on Bach by a fabulous historian and Bach scholar from Yale, Jaroslav Pelikan, in which he asked me to participate. This happened in the early '90s, so it can take a long time for an idea to be realized. Everything has a beginning somewhere and one thing leads to another, though they may not seem connected. It's like the Silk Road—you heard our demonstration of the Project at Columbia University, didn't you?

Yes, and I found it fascinating, both the instruments and the players.

We just wanted to show people what to expect when we do the program at Carnegie Hall in May 2002; there will also be recordings, festivals, even a nifty Web site. When I talk to people on my concert tours and study their cultures and musical instruments, I always come away with many questions in my head. One of these is the idea of culture as a transnational influence, and the Silk Road, though basically a trade route, also connected the cultures of the peoples who used it. To launch the Project, we decided to form a nonprofit, knowledge-based organization that would combine new and traditional information about places where people have been making exciting, wonderful music.

When you learn something from people or from a culture, you accept it as a gift, and it is your lifelong commitment to preserve it and build on it. But an innovation, to grow organically from within, has to be based on an intact tradition, so our idea is to bring together musicians who represent all these traditions, in workshops, festivals, and concerts, to see how we can connect with each other in music.

How do you find them?

We did a lot of field work; Ted Levin, our executive director and a wonderful ethnomusicologist, and others went to Central Asia, China, and Mongolia; located composers and listened to their works; and just yesterday we heard more compositions from Armenia, Turkey, India, Pakistan, Japan, and Korea. Then about two years ago, we asked 16 people to write pieces, and last summer, we invited about 60 musicians to Tanglewood for a 12-day workshop to play them. They came from Iran, Uzbekestan, Tajikistan, China, and Mongolia, but many master performers can also be found in Toronto, Chicago, and San Francisco, and there is a large contingent in Queens, New York. They keep up a strong tradition of their native music, even though, like many emigrants, they often have to do other things to make a living.

Did your 60 musicians speak English?

Some did; language is a problem we have to address. A lot of the Central Asians know Russian, and Ted Levin speaks it fluently. I speak Chinese, but Mongolian is completely different, so we had to have translators.

Are you including Western music in your programs?

Of course—that's the whole idea. Music has always been transnational; people pick up whatever interests them, and certainly a lot of classical music has absorbed influences from all over the world. Take Mahler's "Das Lied von der Erde." When Mahler

Zhao Jiping (left), Wu Man (center), and Yo-Yo Ma at the Silk Road Project Workshop.

developed heart trouble, a friend gave him a book of Chinese poetry called *The Chinese Flute,* and it interested him enough to use it for "Das Lied." Now we want to perform it in Chinese and are having the texts translated back.

Mahler didn't go to Java or Bali or Malaysia, but Bartók did go to Turkey and talked to Turkish composers; Stravinsky claimed he never went to a traditional Russian wedding, but it later turned out that he did. You can hear all these influences in their music, and seeking out their sources has certainly opened up my ears.

In March, I am playing a concerto with the New York Philharmonic that was inspired by the Project and written for me by Richard Danielpour . . .

. . . whose music you've performed before.

That's right. He is Iranian-American, and when he was a child, his grandmother sang Persian songs to him. He remembers a lot of them, and when he was writing this piece, he asked her to sing them again. The concerto includes a part for the kamancheh, the Persian spiked fiddle, which will be played by Kayhan Kalhor, a fabulous Iranian musician and composer, who studied in Canada and divides his time between New York and Teheran. He was among the people who came to Tanglewood, and the Project commissioned him to write a piece that we'll play before the Danielpour; it's scored for various Eastern instruments and a string sextet and it's wonderful. Then the orchestra will play Rimsky-Korsakov's *Scheherazade*, a 19th-century Russian view of Persia.

Tell me about some of the Eastern instruments.

The odd-shaped one I played the other day is the Mongolian morin khuur, which means "horse-head fiddle" because of the shape of its scroll. I was given and taught to play it by some Mongolian musicians at Tanglewood. It has two strings, tuned to F and B-flat; each can be used as an open drone—again!—while the other is fingered. But like the Indian fiddle, the sarangi, it has no fingerboard; you play by pulling the strings sideways or rubbing your nail against them. The bow has no screw—you tighten the hair by feel, pulling on it with your fingers. It is held underhand, as with the gamba and the Chinese er-hu, which also has two strings. These instruments were probably the precursors of the viol family.

Learning to play all this new music and all these new instruments also seems to be doing the impossible. Where do you find the time and energy?

Well, my friend Manny Ax says one of the reasons he loves music is that you learn something new every day; that's what keeps us alive. I'm 45 years old and I've been playing since I was 15, professionally since I was about 20. I've spent at least 12 and a half years of my life traveling, and one thing that's very depressing and that I'm determined to avoid is not being able to remember what I did in the course of a year. This means you must have a reason to be in the places to which you go, and you must do only things that you really care about. So I've cut down, not in terms of activity, but in terms of the number of concerts, so I can do all these other things. I've been home a lot this winter and that's good.

Do you still do your master classes?

Sure, everywhere; it's one way to share what I've learned in other places.

Do you ever worry how all these talented, ambitious, hopeful young people will make a living, not to mention a life?

WHAT HE PLAYS

Yo-Yo Ma's bow is a Tourte, and his strings, on all cellos, are Jargar and Spyracore.

He plays a 1733 Montagnana cello from Venice and the 1712 "Davidoff" Stradivarius, which he now uses only for baroque music. He also has two modern instruments: one that Moes & Moes made for him a couple of years ago, and one that he has had only a few months, made by Mario Miralles, an Argentinean who lives outside Los Angeles. "I love the Moes & Moes," says Ma. "I think it's extraordinary. I played on it for about four months last year and would have continued, except that I had to go to Japan where I had to play the Montagana."

Are they the same in size and dimensions?

No; the Montagnana is bigger than the Strad, and the Moes & Moes is in between. It's their own model; they collaborated on the instrument, it's like the child of both of them. I think it's just as important to play new instruments as to play new pieces; the old ones are getting scarcer and the new ones more and more wonderful. We may be coming to a new golden age of instrument making. I also like Miralles' work a lot, though I haven't played his cello in public yet. It takes me a while to get the feel of an instrument.

To me, the most remarkable thing about these cellos is that when I heard you play the Moes & Moes last summer, I had no idea you had a new cello and thought it was one of your Italian instruments. It goes to show that a great player sounds like himself on any instrument.

You want your instrument to sound the best it can.

Yes, that's a big problem. They go to music school and nobody tells them what's out there. They should be prepared to work with other people, teach, contribute to their community, even to apply the discipline and knowledge they've acquired to some other fields and still derive joy from music.

How do you feel about competitions? Have you ever tried one yourself?

I've lost every competition I ever tried—no, that's not true: I won a competition when I was five—that was the highlight of my career. And once I was on a jury, but I'll never do that again.

Wonderful! But why?

Well, first of all, you have to compare people; that's bad enough. Then, you have to judge them by points, which means dissecting something organic, and denying an artistic person the chance to turn a weakness into a strength. And think how many contestants have to lose so that one may win! And people want younger and younger winners, so the pressure on them is enormous. This is their one big chance: if they blow it, they're finished. They must produce, look good, be charming, but also act like normal kids.

I believe that the years between 15 and 20-something are essential to your development; everything you learn during that time is there for you to draw on the rest of your life. If you put all your energy into performing instead of trying to open yourself to experimenting and learning different ways of making music, you'll be a diminished person. And exploring, finding the depth of your own soul and other people's, that's what music is all about.

What's your next project?

I'm going to Hong Kong, China, and Taiwan. I'm going to do something with [guitarist] John Williams. He's written a cello concerto, and solo pieces that I really love, so I think I'm going to learn and record them. I'm going to premiere the Danielpour Concerto in Lyon, where the French silk industry is located, so there's more than one reason to go there. I'm going to Central Asia and to Turkey, where I'll play some new pieces by Turkish composers. Turkey, of course, is culturally so rich that I can't wait to check it out.

About the Contributors

RICHARD DYER

has been the classical music critic of *The Boston Globe* for 25 years. He has written about music in program notes for the Boston Symphony and the Metropolitan Opera, in liner notes for numerous LPs and CDs, and in magazines, newspapers, The New Grove Dictionary of American Music and Musicians, and The Metropolitan Opera Encyclopedia. He was twice a winner of the ASCAP/Deems Taylor Award for distinguished music criticism.

EDITH EISLER

is a violinist, violist, and teacher in New York. She is a corresponding editor for *Strings* magazine and has been writing for the publication since its inception in 1986. She began studying violin at the age of six in her native Vienna and later studied in Prague, with Max Rostal in London, and with Joseph Fuchs at the Juilliard School in New York. She performed solo and chamber music in Europe and North America and, for 11 years, ran Music among Friends, a series of house concerts performed by New York–based professionals. Of her reviews and profiles of musicians, she says, "Having been on the other side of the footlights most of my life gives me a certain perspective." She also contributes to *Stagebill* and *Chamber Music*, and reviews CDs and books for Amazon.com.

JOHN LEHMANN-HAUPT

a New York–based guitarist and writer, has been playing music since he was five years old. Known equally for his arrangements of popular and traditional songs and for his classical interpretations, he has released recordings on the Physical World and AIG labels. His 12-year engagement at Windows on the World (atop the World Trade Center) was cited by the *New York Times*. Lehmann-Haupt's writings have appeared in the *New York Times* and several other publications, and he is a staff instructor at the American Institute of Guitar.

ANDREW PALMER
a foreign correspondent for *Strings* magazine, lives in Nottingham, England, where he combines dual careers as a freelance writer and a photographer. His work has also appeared on national radio (BBC Radio Three) and the international music press, including *Gramophone*, *Soundscapes* (Australia), *The Flutist Quarterly*, and *Double Reed News*. He is the author of *Divas: In Their Own Words* (The Vernon Press, 2000) and coauthor of Kyra Vayne's autobiography, *A Voice Reborn* (Arcadia Books, 1999).

TIMOTHY PFAFF
is the former editor of *Piano & Keyboard* magazine, music critic for the *San Francisco Examiner* and other U.S. newspapers and magazines, and West Coast correspondent for London's *Financial Times*. A freelance writer on music and other subjects, he currently lives in Laos, where he is writing music reviews for *Tipworld* and working on a book.

BARBARA SEALOCK
is a Cambridge, Massachusetts, writer and journalist. Her work has appeared in *People*, *Boston Magazine*, the *Boston Globe*, the *Christian Science Monitor*, the *Chicago Tribune*, the *Baltimore Sun*, the *New York Daily News*, *Writers' Digest*, *Clavier*, *Strings*, and other publications. She holds a B.A. from Oberlin College.

Acknowledgments

Photographs are used with the kind permission of the following: **pp. vi, 4, 7** by Chad Evans Wyatt courtesy Lois Howard and Associates; **pp. 12, 17** by Waring Abbott courtesy Columbia Artists Management; **p. 18** courtesy Columbia Artists Management; **p. 20** by Steve J. Sherman; **p. 25** by Ian Anderson; **pp. 26, 30, 35** by Marco Borggreve courtesy Channel Classics; **pp. 36, 44, 47** courtesy Kermit Moore; **p. 50** by Beryl Towbin courtesy Lois Jecklin and Associates; **p. 54** courtesy Hai-Ye Ni; **p. 58** by Rory Earnshaw; **pp. 60, 66** courtesy Herbert H. Breslin; **p. 68** courtesy Gurtman and Murtha Associates; **p. 72** by Tania Mara courtesy Askonas Holt Ltd.; **p. 76** courtesy Jian Wang; **p. 81** by Pedro Letria; **pp. 84, 90** by J. Henry Fair courtesy Shirley Kirshbaum and Associates; **pp. 88, 89, 93** courtesy Shirley Kirshbaum and Associates; **p. 96** by Ulrike Welsch courtesy New England Conservatory; **p. 100** by Jeff Thiebauth courtesy New England Conservatory; **p. 101** by Paul Foley courtesy New England Conservatory; **p. 102** by Dorothea Haeften; **pp. 106, 111, 113, 114, 117** by Christian Steiner courtesy Milina Barry, Fine Arts Management; **pp. 120, 130** by Annie Liebowitz courtesy Sony Classical; **p. 129,** by Stu Rosner courtesy Sony Classical.

Other Titles in the Backstage Books Series

Musical Instrument Auction Price Guide, $39.95
Issued annually, illustrated with full-color plates of noteworthy instruments, the *Auction Price Guide* offers the most comprehensive information available on antique and handmade instrument and bow values. A unique five-year summary by instrument and maker of high, low, and average prices show market trends.

Commonsense Instrument Care Guide, $9.95
Violin maker and dealer James N. McKean, past president of the American Federation of Violin and Bow Makers, has written the essential reference on maintaining the playability and value of violins, violas, and cellos and their bows.

Violin Owner's Manual, $14.95 (May 2001)
Read about the defining features of the violin and the evolution of the violin bow. Learn helpful tips on buying and selling, whether it is your first instrument or a major investment. Sound your best with pointers on violin setup, maintenance, repairs, strings, and amplification.

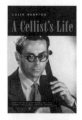

A Cellist's Life, by Colin Hampton, $12.95
One of the 20th century's most distinguished cellists, Colin Hampton is your guide to a bygone world of classical music and musicians. Through his witty, convivial, and candid narrative, you'll encounter such luminaries as Pablo Casals, Ernest Bloch, Igor Stravinsky, Arturo Toscanini, Béla Bartók, and Yehudi Menuhin.

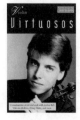

Violin Virtuosos, $12.95
This fascinating companion to Vol. 1 includes profiles of Joshua Bell, Chee-Yun, Kyung-Wha Chung, Jorja Fleezanis, Hilary Hahn, Leila Josefowicz, Mark Kaplan, Viktoria Mullova, Vadim Repin, Joseph Silverstein, and Christian Tetzlaff.